Praise for *The Shift Age*

"The Shift Age is an invaluable compass for aligning the work of complex organizations with the rapidly changing needs and expectations of each organization's stakeholders. Author and futurist David Houle has a knack for 'seeing around corners' in a way that both informs long-term strategic planning and provides a context for day-to-day decision-making. Never has that talent been more essential than it is now. Long before I met David, *The Shift Age* became mandatory reading for executive staff at Winthrop University, and it continues to be a vital orientation resource for new trustees as well."

—Dr. Anthony J. DiGiorgio, President, Winthrop University, Rock Hill, S.C.

"David Houle's *Shift Age* offers an astounding proposition: the Information Age is ending with the emergence of an age of constant change. Read this book!"

—Reese Schonfeld, Co-founder of CNN, CNN Headline News, and Food Network

"*The Shift Age* is a well-written and pivotal book by a sharp-eyed futurist with a gift for being ahead of the curve."

—Richard Noyes, former Associate Director of the Center for Advanced Engineering Study at the Massachusetts Institute of Technology

"Every aspect of our lives is being impacted by the rapid and radical acceleration of technological change. David Houle's important book *The Shift Age* is a fascinating navigational tool that will help guide you as you speed into a future that even our imaginations cannot adequately prepare us to steer through."

—Jack Myers, Editor and Publisher of www.JackMyers.com

"At last a book that explains where we're going and how we got there—written in plain English and designed for short-attention-span readers. Houle writes for all of us who buy more books than we read. After reading just a few of these commentaries, even we luddites can predict what's about to happen and understand the transformations that are now upon us."

—Bob Sirott, NBC5 Chicago News Anchor and WGN Radio Host

"David Houle shares with us such profound thoughts about and a vision for the future of humanity in his recent book, *The Shift Age*. I found the optimism of the human spirit that permeated in this book extremely refreshing. It's an amazing book and a must-read!"

—Dr. Feng Hsu, Senior NASA Engineer, Head of Technical & Technology Risk Assessment and Management at NASA GSFC

"Celebrated futurist David Houle is the perfect guide to show us the next great period of human development. Houle introduces us to *The Shift Age*, the post-Information Age world of global connectedness and individual freedom. To paraphrase another noted futurist, "Fasten your seatbelts, it's going to be a bumpy ride.""

—Charles Memminger, Columnist for the *Honolulu Star-Bulletin* and Author of *Hey Waiter, There's an Umbrella in My Drink!*

"Capturing the dynamics, distress, and decisions we all face, *The Shift Age* is the travel guide for the future."

—Tom Hudson, Managing Editor, First Business TV

"*The Shift Age* is a treasure for those of us who decide what to do on the basis of compelling visions of the future."

—Leo J. Shapiro, Founder and Chairman Emeritus, Leo J. Shapiro & Associates

THE SHIFT SHIFT AGE

DAVID HOULE

Sourcebooks

To Christopher. The future is more yours than mine: may it be bright.

To Victoria. Our future will be filled with love and happiness.

Printed in the United States of America.

RRD 10 9 8 7 6 5 4 3

We should try to be the parents of our future rather than the offspring of our past.

—Miguel de Unamuno (1864–1936),
Spanish essayist, novelist, poet,
playwright, and philosopher

FOREWORD

November 2011

Four years ago, in late 2007, *The Shift Age* was first published. My futurist blog, www.evolutionshift.com, had been up for two years, and I had begun to speak about the Shift Age to audiences in the United States. Outside a growing core of loyal readers of the blog and some early fans, though, I was hardly a known futurist.

In late 2006 and early 2007, with the help of an agent and a well-connected friend in publishing, I circulated a manuscript for a book to publishers (that proposal was for a different book, not *The Shift Age*). As a futurist, though, I felt conflicted approaching the publishing industry at that time, because I had seen what occurred in the media and music industries, and I could clearly see what was about to happen to publishing. (This was the year before the Kindle was announced.) This was an industry that was about to undergo an incredible transformation and disruption—but those in it couldn't see it at the time. In a column that's included in this book (titled "A Book Convention: In the Year 2025" and written in June 2007) I correctly forecasted the explosion of online sales; the radical change in book stores; that there would be electronic book readers that would trigger a huge move to ebooks; and that the age of universal physicality of books was at an end. So as a futurist, it was odd for me to knock on the door of an industry that I was predicting was about to experience massive upheaval.

This soon-to-be-disrupted industry reacted to my manuscript in ways that were ridiculous and laughable. There's no need to go over those here; the reactions weren't personal, just based on soon-to-be-out-of-date thinking. There was one exception, though. Peter Lynch at Sourcebooks really got my book proposal, and presented it to the editorial committee at Sourcebooks. Now the committee would need to unanimously approve my proposal in order to offer publication, and I didn't get a unanimous vote at that time. Sourcebooks clearly got it more than the other publisher did, but perhaps it was just too early.

So I decided to have *The Shift Age* published by BookSurge, the in-house imprint of Amazon. Since Amazon had recently announced the Kindle, The Shift Age was one of the first books on the imprint to be converted to the Kindle ebook format.

Since late 2007, *The Shift Age* has become a highly influential book for CEOs and corporations. I have become known as "the CEO's futurist," having advised or presented to 2,000+ CEOs and business owners. Numerous companies—many of whom I have never met—have told me that this book has inspired them to successfully change their entire business models to face the new realities of the Shift Age. So, while not a bestseller in the traditional publishing metrics, this book has indeed become influential beyond simple sales numbers.

In addition, since this book was published the first time, my speaking career as a futurist has taken off. I have delivered major keynote addresses on six continents and made some four hundred speeches and presentations. This is where my true influence has been, along with my blog and the Shift Age Newsletter.

I am happy to say I have now entered into a wide-ranging and innovative publishing relationship with Sourcebooks (it was unanimous this time) to write books about the future, utilizing a publishing model of the future that isn't tied to the traditional publishing models or timelines. This is the perfect marriage of a futurist and a future-facing publisher. The re-publication of *The Shift Age* in print and digital form is the first step in this relationship. The hope of this author is that the partnership with Sourcebooks will allow *The Shift Age* to reach a larger audience.

Other than this foreword, nothing of substance has been changed in the book. That, in fact, is the point. Many of the columns—all with dates—included here will allow you, the reader, to see the accuracy of my forecasts, predictions and visions of the Shift Age we are now entering. Some notable examples, in addition to the June 2007 column on the future of book publishing, are: "The World Cup Points the Way," where I point to the fact that we are moving to a global society and culture; "It is All Global," which points to the interconnectedness of global finance and its consequences; "Debt, Credit, Obligations and Trust," where I wrote about how the commoditization of mortgages would lead to disruption and that debt would be a troubling global issue through 2013; "Damaged Brands," where I forecasted that "Made in China" and "Wall Street Investment Instruments" would be damaged brands in the years ahead; and "Cell Phones are Transformative," which forecasted that the cell phone would soon be globally ubiquitous and that this connectivity of communication may in fact be a way to view the Mayan Prophesy of 2012.

Perhaps one of the columns I have referred to most often during Q&A sessions after my speeches is "Technology Increases, Privacy Declines," written in 2006, before social media reached hundreds of millions of users. People always ask me about privacy, and, after sourcing this column, I say that the definition of privacy is mutable and that what was considered privacy twenty, thirty or one hundred years ago has been rendered obsolete by technology.

Perhaps some of my most prescient columns are in the chapter on disintermediation, where I speak about how much the Internet will disrupt existing models. As I write this foreword, a column that jumps out is "The Political Party: A Candidate for Disintermediation." In it, I write that the two-party system will soon be irrelevant in the United States, and in this transformative Shift Age, might be replaced or reinvented.

All of these columns are in Part Two of this book and are grouped by subject. Please feel free to jump around as you like and as your interests dictate.

Part One of this book sets down the basic concepts, ideas and visions of the Shift Age—the age we are now in. Please read this section first to gain the larger context of the age.

I look forward to enlarging and expanding upon *The Shift Age* in my new relationship with Sourcebooks, as it is definitely a Shift Age publisher. And once you finish the book, I hope you will embrace opportunities of the Shift Age as well, in your work and in your life.

Welcome to the Shift Age!

CONTENTS

Preface xiii

Introduction xv

Part I: The Shift Age 1

  Chapter 1: The Shift Age in Context 3

  Chapter 2: The Threshold Decades 7

  Chapter 3: The Shift Age 23

Part II: Commentary on the Shift Age 43

  Introduction 45

  Chapter 4: Going Global 47

    Exit Greenspan, the Economist's Rock Star 47

    The World Cup Points the Way 50

    Made in China 52

    It Is All Global 54

    Debt, Credit, Obligations, and Trust 56

    Damaged Brands 59

  Chapter 5: Technology and Transformation 63

    Sometimes It Is Easy to See the Future:
      A Futuristic Pocketful 63

    Happy Birthday, PC! 66

Sometimes It Is Easy to See the Future:

    Head to the Beach for a Day at Work..........................68

Always Faster..........................70

Sometimes It Is Easy to See the Future:

    Is It Real?..........................72

Cell Phones Are Transformative..........................74

The Future of Video Games..........................77

Technology Advances, Privacy Declines..........................80

Berkeley and Nanotechnology..........................81

A Cell Phone Milestone..........................83

Moore's Law Lives On..........................85

The iPhone Starts It Up Again..........................87

A New Cell Phone Milestone..........................89

Chapter 6: Energy and Global Warming..........................91

Solving the Energy Problem and Saving Ourselves..........................92

Europe All the Time, New York When It Needs To..........................96

A Walk on the Beach..........................98

Once Again It Starts in California..........................100

National Defense Becomes Green..........................102

Make Global Warming an Economic Issue..........................104

Three Cheers for Titanium Dioxide..........................106

A Man Who Is Working to Save the Planet..........................107

We Have Only Just Begun..........................111

Change the Language, Change the Thinking..........................113

Sputnik: 50 Years Later..........................116

Contents

Chapter 7: Our Automotive Future 121

An Electric Car 122

A Man Who Wants to Change the World 125

The Quest for the Perfect Battery: Part One 128

The Quest for the Perfect Battery: Part Two 130

The Compressed Air Car 133

Chapter 8: A Time of Disintermediation 137

Disintermediation: A Buzzword to Bring Back 137

Disintermediation: A Deeper Look 141

Watching Video, Selling a Home, Buying Insurance 143

The Political Party in the United States:
  A Candidate for Disintermediation? 149

Guilty Pleasures 152

Disintermediation Is Rarely Partial 154

Say Good-bye to the 6-percent Commission Rule 155

**Chapter 9: Intellectual Property, the Wealth
of the Shift Age** 159

Intellectual Property Is the New Valuation 159

A Historic Day for Intellectual Property 162

The Financial Exchange for the 21st Century 165

The Merchant Banker of Intellectual Capital 168

Chapter 10: The Morphing of Media 175

Broadband...Finally! 176

High-touch Media 180

A Media Milestone 183

Three Deaths of a Media Icon 184

A Book Convention: In the Year 2025 187

Chapter 11: Culture at the Beginning of the Shift Age 191

In the Future, Let's All Get Caught Napping 191

Coffee and Caffeine 194

The New Coffee Culture and Why It
Reflects Our Changing World 196

New and Threatening Becomes Acceptable
and Mainstream 199

Water 201

Water Redux 203

A 20th-century Habit 205

Time Capsule for 2057 208

Expanding the Definition of Life 210

A Happiness Index 212

2007: Looking Back and Looking Forward 214

Notes 217

Acknowledgments 223

About the Author 227

PREFACE

THIS BOOK IS a product of a life lived slightly ahead of the curve.

All of us, at some point in our lives, recognize themes or patterns that seem to represent who we are and what we have become. I have become someone who thinks about the future: a future-thinker, or a futurist. I am attracted to newness, to discovery, to finding out what is around the corner. In hindsight I see that I have often been ahead of the curve.

I spent the better part of 1970 and 1971 living in a VW Microbus I'd configured into an extremely compact living space (perhaps the only significant handyman accomplishment in my life). I traveled all over Canada, the United States, and Mexico, parking in campgrounds, in forests, on beaches, and on city streets. Two years later I read in a variety of newspapers and national magazines that the newest trend was outfitting vans to live and travel in. One year after the van experience, I took off for what became a year-long backpacking trip around the world, visiting Morocco, Turkey, Iran, Afghanistan, India, Nepal, Burma, Malaysia, Laos, Hong Kong, and Japan. Later that decade the media started to discuss the new phenomenon of global backpackers.

Professionally I was part of the executive team that launched MTV. I started work six months before the launch of the network. This was in the earliest days of cable, 1981, and everyone thought I was nuts to leave CBS.

I distinctly remember thinking that, for the 20 years prior, two of the most dominant cultural forces in America had been television and rock and roll, so how could this miss? I stayed long enough to help in the launch of Nickelodeon, VH1, and CNN Headline News.

As a student of media, it became clear to me in the early 1990s that the network television business was about to undergo disruptive change. New competition and distribution models were going to be introduced that would forever change the business practices of the industry. Since distribution, and therefore audiences, would change, the constants would be the content, or programs, and advertising. I co-founded and co-developed a consortium of network advertisers to fund network programming, matching advertisers with high-quality programs. Initially successful, the business model was implemented throughout the advertising industry in the decade that followed. The vision that was the impetus for that initial effort—and much resisted at the time—is now the reality of the media marketplace.

Being slightly ahead of the curve is not always a comfortable place to be. People doubt the vision; they are caught up in past models, present lives, and conventional thinking. A quote that has always kept me going and given me strength is the wonderful comment by Arthur Schopenhauer: "In the revelation of any truth there are three stages. First it is ridiculed. Second it is resisted. In the third it is considered self-evident."

INTRODUCTION

THREE YEARS AGO I set out to write a book about the future; you hold the result in your hands. The goal was to present a clear picture of the current dynamics shaping our world and to then project them forward to suggest what may lie ahead.

The thesis of Part of I of this book is that humanity is entering a new age, the Shift Age, which will be a time of great transformation for us all. As this thesis took shape, an avalanche of corroborating evidence confirmed my belief. Developments in many areas of human endeavor clearly pointed the way.

While the longer trend lines needed more research, the more immediate manifestations of these trends were everywhere. The desire to comment on them was the genesis of my futurist blog (http://www.evolutionshift.com) that has as its tagline "A Future Look at Today." Two or three times a week I post columns that discuss news, events, and trends. Launched in early 2006, this blog quickly developed a loyal readership. Now, some 200 posts later, many of these columns are included in Part II of this book, grouped by general subject matter into chapters. These groupings and the editing they have undergone should make them fresh to even the most regular readers of the Evolution Shift blog. They provide commentary on the Shift Age, reporting from the front lines, as we move into a time of great change, much risk, and the promise of a new golden era for humanity.

We live in an age of information and media overload, which influences how we read books. Over the past three years I have had discussions with numerous people about how they read the books they buy. Many people were frustrated they were not able to read more because of the other demands on their time. Many admitted they bought more books than they read. Others would start long books but never finish them because so much of their reading had to be done in short bursts that the thread of the book was lost. I often heard that books need to be written so they can be consumed in the staccato rhythm of an "always on" life. I took these comments into account in writing this book. Most chapters are short, and the longer chapters are comprised of short chunks. Most of the columns in Part II can be read in 5 to 10 minutes. I hope you make the commitment to read the entire book. Know that it has been structured so that you can.

Finally, this will be the first of several books about the Shift Age and the future. I plan to expand upon and go deeper into some of the bigger concepts and trends of this new age with a follow-up Shift Age book. Then I plan to have a book published on the 2010-2020 decade, which could well be one of the single most transformative decades in human history. There might also be a third book that looks at a probable monumental transformation in human consciousness that could well usher humanity into a new golden age. These books, as they are about the future, may well be published in new ways and formats. So stay tuned, as we face the future together.

PART I:
THE SHIFT AGE

CHAPTER 1:
THE SHIFT AGE IN CONTEXT

W E NOW LIVE in the Shift Age, a time of transformation that will be regarded by future historians as one of the most significant periods in human history. How we navigate these next 20 to 30 years will determine whether these future historians praise our perspicacity or wonder why we failed to grasp the evolutionary imperatives so obvious to them.

As the world entered the final quarter of the 20th century, it became clear that one age was giving way to another. While the new age was not yet fully formed, its early manifestations suggested a clear direction. The massive increase in college graduates in the United States due first to the GI Bill post World War II (officially, the Servicemen's Readjustment Act of 1944) and then to the baby boomer generation, the transformation of the workforce from blue- to white-collar, the advent of computers and their migration into everyday life, and the launch of communications satellites all presaged the onset of something new.

From the vantage point of the Industrial Age, it appeared that this new age was about information, so the coming time was christened the Information Age by scholars, futurists, and historians alike. This name became part of the vernacular and has been used to define our time ever since. The great future-thinker and historian Alvin Toffler called it the Third Wave, following the previous waves of industry and agriculture. These terms are now some 30 years old, and during this time the speed of change has only accelerated. Unexpected transformation has occurred. It is time to give the age we live in a new name because it is a different place than what it was projected to be by those who gave the Information Age its name decades ago.

Welcome to the Shift Age.

A Brief, Brief History of Humanity Leading to the Shift Age

IT IS GENERALLY accepted that the age of modern man began around 150,000 years ago. For most of this time, humanity scarcely differed from other animals—simply trying to survive day to day by hunting and gathering. Then, approximately 10,000 years ago, some groups of humans started to literally put down roots, and the Agricultural Age began. This led to the placed-based development of society and culture. Most of the history of humanity and certainly all of its developed civilizations came into being during this time. The basic foundation of human society was developed during the Agricultural Age.

The Agricultural Age continued until the 1700s, when the invention of the steam engine ushered in the Industrial Age, which spanned roughly 250 years until, in the last quarter of the 20th century, the Information Age began in developed countries.

Accept for the sake of simple arithmetic that a human lifetime is 50 years. That means the time man has existed in current form, 150,000 years, is approximately 3,000 lifetimes. The Agricultural Age, 10,000 years in length, represents 200 lifetimes. So for 2,800 of modern man's lifetimes he was essentially nomadic and lived in portable housing or in caves. For 200 lifetimes he tilled the land and created civilization, and for only 5 lifetimes he lived in the Industrial Age, with machines. Finally it is during the life of most adults alive today that modern man has lived in the Information Age.

Modern man therefore has spent 2,800 lifetimes in caves, 200 lifetimes tilling the land, 5 lifetimes with machines, and only a single lifetime living in the Information Age. When we look at our species in the context of this timeline, it is clear that most of what we think of when we think of "humanity" and "society" is recent.

During the first 2,800 lifetimes, humanity had no sense of the speed of change. Survival was the only issue. Even during the Agricultural Age, the speed of change was hardly noticeable in a lifetime. People lived in the same place and held the same occupation as their parents. In the last few centuries of this age, exploration and discovery started to accelerate the social, cultural, and economic evolution of humanity around the world. The Renaissance in Europe, the great Mayan and Aztec civilizations of Central America, and the sophisticated dynasties in China all were toward the end of the Agricultural Age. Even during these great strides forward, humans had little or no concept of change in a lifetime. It was not until the beginning of the Industrial Age that the quickness of change was experienced by humans on a large scale.

In the United States, for example, if you were born in the year 1825, you grew up in an essentially agricultural society. The majority of the population lived in the country or small towns, and land and products from it determined wealth. By your 60th birthday, manufacturing began to supplant farming, cities underwent explosive growth, you traveled by train, and you could have your photograph taken. The world you lived in was noticeably different than that of your grandparents and even parents.

My grandparents grew up in a world of steam engines, candlelight, and horse and buggy. I grew up in a world of television, jet planes, and communication satellites. My son grew up with video games, computers, cell phones, digital media, and the Internet. Therefore, it is only in the last five or six lifetimes of humanity's time on earth that the speed of change could be clearly perceived by a majority of the population. This is essential to remember, as the awareness and experience of the speed of change as a phenomenon is common to practically every human alive today.

It is generally accepted that the Industrial Age began in the 1700s and that the Information Age began sometime between 1950 and 1980. Clearly there is no one date but a period of transition between any two historical epochs or ages. For the sake of consistency and clarity and because I believe the demarcation between these two ages became clear in the middle of the 1970s, I use the date of 1975 to mark the beginning of the Information Age.

Since the Information Age began approximately 30 years ago in developed countries, the perception of change and the speed of change have become pronounced. The future seems to show up in our lives at an accelerating rate. Alvin Toffler's book *Future Shock* was published in 1970; in the decades since then, humanity has come to accept this future shock as an almost constant experience. We settle into learning and adapting to a new technology and its enabling power in our lives, and then almost immediately a new technological breakthrough or gadget renders what we just mastered dated or even obsolete. We embrace innovation, and yet, at times, it overwhelms us. All of us, to some degree, have experienced innovation fatigue. We want to keep up, and in most areas of our lives we do, but there always seems to be a part of our lives where we can't quite catch up. Things move at us too fast and with great force, as though we're drinking from a fire hose. This sense of the rapidity of change really began in the past 20 years, a transitional time when humanity moved from what was to what will be. I call these 20 years the Threshold Decades.

CHAPTER 2:
THE THRESHOLD DECADES: 1985 TO 2005

threshold

1: the plank, stone, or piece of timber that lies under a door: sill

2 a: gate, door b (1): end, boundary; *specifically:* the end of a runway (2): the place or point of entering or beginning: outset <on the *threshold* of a new age>

3 a: the point at which a physiological or psychological effect begins to be produced <has a high *threshold* for pain> b: a level, point, or value above which something is true or will take place and below which it is not or will not

— Merriam-Webster Online Dictionary

THE YEARS FROM 1985 to 2005 were a time of incredible change. In fact, it is hard to find another 20-year period in the history of humanity when our world changed as much as during this time. Fifty years from now, I believe these two decades will be seen as a true demarcation in the history of humanity, an obvious time bridge between two eras. As the dictionary states, a threshold is a place of entering or beginning. It is a place between two rooms, a doorway. Threshold is also used regarding pain, as in one's "pain threshold." All three meanings pertain to the Threshold Decades, the 20-year period from 1985 to 2005.

Practically every aspect of life changed. Since there has been so much transformation, change, and innovation, it is easy to forget what actually happened during these 20 years. Here is a quick look at 1985. The political and economic world was divided in two: the Eastern Bloc, controlled by the Soviet Union, and the Western Bloc, led by the United States. China was the world's largest communist nation, with closed and protected borders. The precursor to the Internet was used by a few thousand people, mostly in scientific, academic, and governmental settings. The first cell phones were appearing. They weighed several pounds, and there were just a few hundred thousand users. The personal computer was in the very early stages of distribution and existed mostly in business settings. The fax machine was just gaining wide distribution. There were three broadcast networks in the United States. The penetration of cable television in the United States was under 40 percent, and there were fewer than 20 cable networks.

On a more personal note, if you were a middle-class American, you had a repressed fear of a nuclear war with the Soviet Union. You had a phone at home and one at the office, both attached to the wall. You probably had in your entire office complex one or two personal computers that somebody had been specially trained to operate. There might have been a single, slow fax machine in your workplace. You watched one of the three broadcast networks, and, if you were among the fortunate 40 percent of the country that had cable TV, you had an additional 9 to 20 channels. You might have been in the 40 percent of the population that had a VCR, but most of what you viewed you recorded (with difficulty) as there were few video rental stores. You listened to music on vinyl records or audio cassettes. You rarely experienced what is now called "airport security." You most likely had never heard of AIDS or HIV, and you had certainly never heard of Al-Qaeda, outsourcing, downsizing, cheap airfares, DNA mapping, or the Internet.

Explosive Growth in Technological Connectedness

THE THRESHOLD DECADES were not only a period of time of fundamental change, it was also a time when technologies developed and brought to market in the previous decades experienced explosive growth.

Number (Worldwide)	1950	1975	1985	1995	2005
Computers	60	650,000	50,000,000	200,000,000	822,150,000
Cell Phone Subscribers			700,000	89,000,000	2,065,000,000
Internet Users			21,000	45,100,000	1,081,000,000

Figure 1. Global Technology Growth: 1950 to 2005.[1]

Number (in the U.S.)	1950	1975	1985	1995	2005
Computers	9	400,000	30,000,000	80,000,000	223,810,000
Cell Phone Subscribers			340,000	34,000,000	202,000,000
Internet Users			19,000	28,100,000	210,000,000

Figure 2. Technology Growth in the United States: 1950 to 2005.[2]

The exponential growth in number of computers between 1975 and 1985 was largely due to the introduction of the first personal computers. Before this time, most computers were mainframes or mini-computers used exclusively by institutions. As these numbers indicate, the Threshold Decades were clearly a time when computers went from being something special for businesses to being commonplace and for everyone.

The truly remarkable numbers in figures 1 and 2 are those regarding cell phones and Internet use. Both technologies went from early stage to full market penetration and acceptance, providing electronic connectedness to the world.

At the beginning of the Threshold Decades, in 1985, humanity was not connected except via landline phones, and it was only in developed countries where these landlines were used by a majority of households. In 2005, more than two billion people had cell phones; not only were there more phones in use around the world, but they were portable. Communication ceased to be tied to place as it had been in 1985. This is an extremely important transition as it made human communication completely mobile for the first time in history. People could be anywhere and be connected. More people connected, more of the time, always available. While the United States represented close to 50 percent of all cell phones in 1985, that percentage was down to 10 percent in 2005. The cell phone has become a global technology.

The growth in Internet usage was even greater. In 1985 the Internet was not available to the public, so all traffic was institutional. By 2005 the increasing connectedness of the world collapsed time and distance in the realm of human communication. This connectedness was simultaneous and parallel to the massive social, political, and economic forces that were unleashing globalism around the world. It is interesting to note that, as with cell phones, the United States was dominant in Internet usage in 1985, with 90 percent of all users, but by 2005 that percentage had dropped to 20 percent. The world was quickly adapting to this new 24/7 electronic medium. The transformation was creating a "global village" vaster and more interactive than anything Marshall McLuhan, the man who coined the phrase in the 1960s, could have foreseen.

The electronic communications global village created during the Threshold Decades was not due just to the exponential growth in the number of users of cell phones, the Internet, and computers. The constant innovation in all these technologies was an ongoing phenomenon. Moore's Law—the theory developed by Gordon Moore, founder of Intel in 1965, that states that computing power and speed doubles every 18 months[3] while at the same time drops in price by half—became a living reality.

Every year or two there was a new generation of computers that were smaller, faster, more powerful, and cheaper. This not only fed the rapid growth of the PC market, it also dramatically increased speed and productivity in business. As computer capability dramatically increased, it affected the explosive growth of Internet usage as the download speeds for modem dial-up increased every year. Paralleling this was the miniaturization of cell phones that were increasingly feature-rich. By 2005 PCs, cell phones, cell phone contracts, and access to the Internet had dropped in price so much compared to even a few years earlier that all these technologies became commodities. The cell phone went from being a cutting-edge, transformative, expensive piece of technology to being a disposable consumer product. All of this greatly affected usage patterns.

The following graphs give visual snapshots of these developments, which began and exploded between 1985 and 2005. (Numbers are actual to 2005 and projected beyond.) Please keep in mind that the global numbers and percentages include the entire world—developed, developing, and undeveloped countries.

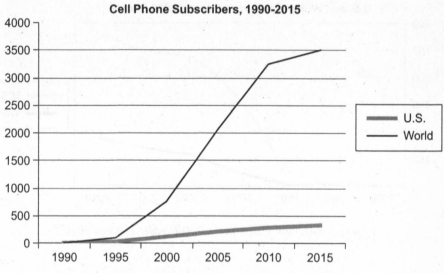

Figure 3. Cell Phone Subscribers: 1990 to 2015.[4]

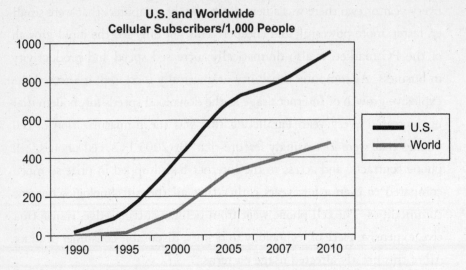

Figure 4. Cell Phone Subscribers per 1,000 People: 1990 to 2010.[5]

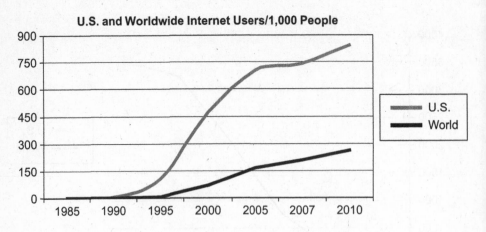

Figure 5. Internet Usage per 1,000 People: 1985 to 2010.[6]

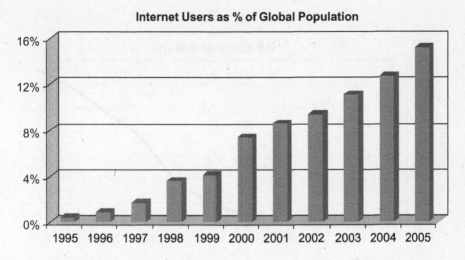

Figure 6. *Internet Users as a Percent of Global Population: 1995 to 2005.*[7]

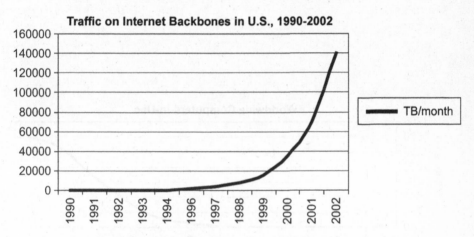

Figure 7. *Traffic, in Terabytes, on Internet Backbones in the United States: 1990 to 2002.*[8]

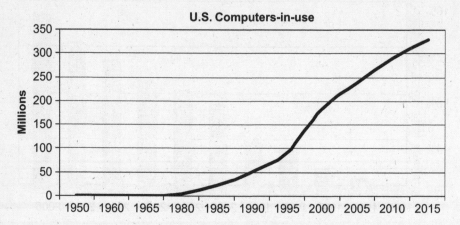

Figure 8. Computers in Use in the United States: 1950 to 2015.[9]

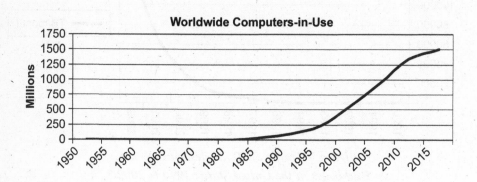

Figure 9. Computers in Use Worldwide: 1950 to 2015.[10]

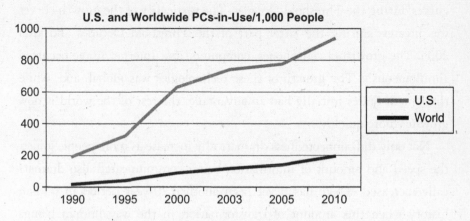

Figure 10. Personal Computers per 1,000 People: 1990 to 2010.[11]

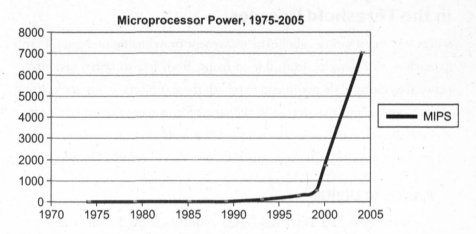

Figure 11. Microprocessor Power in MIPS
(Million Instructions per Second): 1975 to 2005.[12]

There are several key points conveyed in these graphs. All three technologies—cell phones, Internet, and PCs—display accelerating growth curves during the Threshold Decades. The verticality of the growth curves was greatest during the latter part of the Threshold Decades and after 2005. The growth of cell phones, computers, and Internet usage occurred simultaneously. The growth of these technologies was global, and, while the United States initially had an advantage, the rest of the world is now growing more quickly.

Not only did connectedness dramatically increase as more people joined, the speed and amount of information being communicated also dramatically increased. There has never been another 20-year period in human history when this amount of transformation in the way human beings communicate with each other has occurred. In this regard, the Threshold Decades represent a singular time in history. A level of human connectedness now exists that is not only new but that was practically unthinkable decades ago, except perhaps in the pages of science fiction.

Other Major Transformations in the Threshold Decades

MUCH HAS BEEN written about the movement from analog to digital, from hierarchies to networks, from few to many, from fast to faster, and from regional to global. I do not intend to rehash these subjects—this book, after all, is a book about macro trends, the larger forces reorganizing our world, and the direction they are taking us—but a brief recap is constructive to set the stage for the Shift Age, which follows the Threshold Decades.

Analog to Digital

Between 1985 and 2005 developed countries moved from analog to digital. This shift underpins the technological communications growth and computing explosion cited above. It is also evidenced in music moving from analog LPs and tapes to CDs to digital downloading. The same parallel occurred in film with the move from VHS to DVD to digital downloading. Digital downloading greatly increased Internet use, caused upheaval in the affected industries, and disintermediated professions.

The conversion to digital also accelerated access and usage. A consumer can go right to her favorite song on the CD or scene on the DVD, without waiting for fast-forwarding. This has created an expectation among consumers of immediacy and "on demand" fulfillment.

Hierarchies to Networks

In 1985 the world was still largely structured around hierarchies. The drive toward centralization that occurred during the Industrial Age created large hierarchies in business, government, and practically any large organization. In fact, half of the world, the Eastern Bloc, operated with central planning committees. Even in the social realm, there were pecking orders, remnants of the aristocracies of the Agricultural Age, and economic social structures held over from the robber barons of the Industrial Age.

These hierarchies were challenged and, in many cases, converted or obliterated during the Threshold Decades, when most of society started to reorganize around the network structure. Vertical hierarchies flattened into horizontal networks. Decision-making was pushed down in organizations, rendering hierarchy less important. The new connectedness allowed people to circumvent traditional social structures and connect around common interests, regardless of location. In 1985 people worked up the corporate ladder and socialized at private clubs. In 2005 people worked as independent contractors or entrepreneurs, connecting on social networks such as MySpace.

Our world is now one of networks. Hierarchies still exist, but they are no longer as respected and are often scorned for being slow-moving.

Few to Many: The Triumph of Choice

Along with the transition from hierarchies to networks came the shift from few to many. Even on the political front, numbers increased. In 1985 there were 159 member nations of the United Nations. In 2005 there were 191, largely due to the fragmenting of the Soviet Union into 15 countries and Yugoslavia into 5.

Media is perhaps the clearest example of the explosion of choice. In 1985 the United States had 3 broadcast networks and approximately 20 cable networks. In 2005 there were 6 broadcast networks and more than 100 cable networks. The number of Web sites went from a handful to millions.

Number (in the United States)	1950	1975	1985	1995	2005
Radio Stations	2,232	4,463	8,593	11,987	13,499
Web Sites			0	no data available	71,000,000 (estimated)
Published Books	11,022	39,372	75,452	113,589	172,005
TV Channels (Average Household)	2	3	18	41	102

Figure 12. The Explosion of Choice in the United States: 1950 to 2005.[13]

While this movement from few to many occurred, new technologies came to market that helped the consumer make selections. During the growth of television-viewing options, the remote control came to market: the viewer could change channels without getting up from the couch. This was the beginning of the end of network programmers' command over viewers. As choice increased, a new technology, the remote control, helped the consumer make fast and immediate decisions. This also happened with the digital purchase of music, allowing the buyer to select single tracks and therefore unbundle the album concept of music.

The key development that came from the transition of few to many was the explosion of choice for everyone. With hundreds of channels, tens of thousands of books, millions of Web sites, and even dozens of different toothpastes, the consumer has an ever-increasing amount of choice and therefore control. Today more than any time in history, the consumer has the power of choice and uses that power every day.

Ever Faster

During the Threshold Decades everything seemed to move faster and faster. Cell phones, the Internet, and personal computers drove this acceleration. The back-and-forth nature of most human communication collapsed. The turnaround time for mailing a letter and receiving a response was approximately a week; the turnaround time for sending and receiving an e-mail was minutes, and instant messaging only took seconds. The speed of computers doubled every two years or less. Waiting for someone to get home or get to the office to return a phone call was no longer necessary; you called the person wherever she was. This time-shortening increased the velocity of transactions, business decisions, and plans (teenagers now make plans moment to moment via text messaging). Decisions happened much faster in a networked, decentralized environment than in a hierarchical, centralized one. Work could be done much more quickly on faster computers.

When Internet usage took off during the second half of the Threshold Decades, people could work around the clock. Suffer from insomnia in the middle of the night? Send e-mails. Financial projections need to be reworked? Have them back on the boss's electronic desk before she logs on in the morning.

Work became something one could do 24/7. Communications became closer to immediate than ever before. All this connectedness accelerated human interaction. Factor in the constant and rapid rate of innovation across numerous fields: medicine, science, non-human space exploration, artistic creation, most forms of content publishing, and any number of other fields underwent significant advancement, accelerating the general speed of change to a rate never before experienced.

By the end of the Threshold Decades, the speed of change had accelerated so much that it was no longer sequential as in the Industrial Age but had become simultaneous across multiple social areas. This set the stage for the Shift Age, where change becomes part of our environment.

West Meets East

The social, economic, and political ramifications of the unification of the Eastern Bloc and the Western Bloc cannot be overstated. In 1985 communism was perceived as a possible economic and political order. By 2005 it was essentially dead as a viable way of governance. In 1985 there was no real global economy. In 2005 there was a global economy. The largest communist country in the world, China, became the fastest growing capitalistic economy in the world. In 1985 there was minimal and highly controlled economic activity between the Eastern and Western Blocs. In 2005 Europe used millions of barrels of Russian oil, and the United States was awash in products made in China. The collapse of communism, most symbolically represented by the tearing down of the Berlin Wall, created a vacuum, and global forces rushed in. For the first time since before World War I, the economic movement toward a global economy resumed and then took off.

There was another merger of East and West that was equally profound, although perhaps less noticeable. This was the merger of underlying beliefs and philosophies. During the second half of the 20th century, culminating during the Threshold Decades, Western science, particularly in the fields of particle and quantum physics, reached several core conclusions. Drilling down into ever-smaller subatomic particles, physicists realized that everything, at its core, is energy.

For centuries, Eastern philosophy and religion were based on the belief that everything was energy. Finally, as predicted by several thinkers who had bridged Eastern and Western thinking, the two schools of thought ended up at the same place: All is One.

Not only had the economic, political, and social barriers to the movement to global order come to an end during the Threshold Decades, a partial unification of the underlying tenets of Western scientific thought and Eastern philosophical thought had come together. The obvious cultural manifestation of this in the United States and Europe was the explosive growth of such practices as yoga and meditation and the Dalai Lama and Deepak Chopra scaling the bestseller lists. Humanity was on the path to becoming one.

In summary, the Threshold Decades were a time of transformative change. The human landscape was so altered that the door closed on what had been and swung wide open on what will be. The world moved from Industrial Age values through Information Age values to the dawn of another age just beginning. Let's now take a look at where we find ourselves: the Shift Age.

CHAPTER 3:
THE SHIFT AGE

T HE INCREDIBLE CHANGE that occurred during the Threshold Decades laid the foundation for a new age. While this new age may still look like the Information Age, it will soon take on clear and unique characteristics.

The Information Age lasted from about 10 years before the Threshold Decades until where we are now, the transition to the Shift Age. Much as the first 10 years of the Information Age, from 1975 to 1985, were powerfully influenced by the Industrial Age, the years from 2005 to 2010 are the transition from the Information Age to the Shift Age.

While ages and stages of history blend into each other, there are simple conceptual characteristics to every age.

- Tools defined the Agricultural Age.
- Machines defined the Industrial Age.
- Technology defined the Information Age.
- Consciousness will define the Shift Age.

Clearly, in the year 2007 and for the foreseeable future, technology will continue to be a major influence in the world. This is no different than the continuing importance of tools and machines in today's world. There are tools still in use that were invented during the Agricultural Age. The same goes for Industrial Age machines. Each age adds to what has gone before, expanding and accelerating the human experience. The consciousness that will occur in the Shift Age will continue this expansion and acceleration.

Speed of Change

IN THE SHIFT Age the speed of change is becoming part of our environment. During most of the Agricultural Age the speed of change was hardly noticeable. In the Industrial Age the speed of change became sequential. One invention set the stage for another. The invention of the telegraph, for example, led to the invention of the telephone. The speed of change started to palpably accelerate in the 18th century. Things moved more quickly in the 20th century than in the 19th. In the course of a human lifetime amazing change occurred. My father was born into a world where there was only limited use of radio; it had yet to become a mass medium. At the time of his death, three years after the introduction of the Web browser, the Internet was rapidly becoming a mass medium.

During the Information Age, and especially the Threshold Decades, the speed of change accelerated even further. It moved from being sequential to being simultaneous. All of us, at one time or another during this period, were overwhelmed by change, newness, or a sense of not being able to keep up, to stay current. This acceleration started sooner in developed countries than in less-developed countries. This dizzying feeling of speed was initially felt in the United States, Japan, Korea, and Western Europe, where innovation and the rapid growth of technology and communications first occurred. Less-developed countries soon followed, and it was in these areas that this speed of change was shocking. Countries that were still largely agricultural or developing early-stage manufacturing went from being rural, with little or no communications infrastructure, directly to the digital age, leapfrogging the historical process of developed countries. The dramatic acceleration of the speed of change was then global, with the fastest speeds in developing countries.

The speed of change in the Shift Age is a through line that can no longer be measured; it has actually become part of our environment. Change is the context in which we live. We feel it. We see it. We are constantly confronted with change. We cannot keep up. We must always adapt. Three-year business plans are laughable. Even three-month business plans in certain industries are challenged.

We sometimes feel disoriented because of this ever-present, accelerating speed of change; things no longer seem to be fixed but rather in an ongoing state of flux. An appropriate metaphor for the Shift Age is an earthquake. If you have experienced an earthquake, you know the sense of powerlessness. The first feeling is disorientation: what is this? Recognition that this is an earthquake instills fear, then prompts reaction. What to do? What can I do? Then comes the realization that second-to-second attention to personal safety is the only possible focus as one is powerless to do anything else. The ground is literally shifting underfoot. You survive but are shaken. You experience turbulence you can't control, and yet you come out the other side—but with a different outlook on your life and of life in general. Welcome to the Shift Age.

The Three Forces of the Shift Age

EVERY AGE IS ushered in and shaped by a confluence of forces that disrupt and alter society. Computers, communications satellites, a knowledge-based economy, and the move from analog to digital all helped shape the Information Age. What are the forces that are shaping the Shift Age?

Three overarching forces are shaping the Shift Age:

- Accelerating electronic connectedness
- The flow to global
- The flow to individual

Of course, there are many dynamics and influences defining our world here in the early part of this new millennium: religious fundamentalism, geopolitical issues such as energy, poverty, migration, resource allocation, and population growth. But these three forces—accelerating electronic connect-edness, the flow to global, and the flow to individual—are the underlying, essential, irresistible energy flows that announce a new age in humanity's evolution, a reorganization of global society that rivals any in history.

Accelerating Electronic Connectedness

Overview

Accelerating electronic connectedness, as we have seen, took off during the Threshold Decades. This force, particularly in its Internet manifestation, has been much written about and certainly widely experienced. This con-nectedness, happening at the speed of light via fiber optics, is creating an entire new place: the neurosphere.[1] The earth's biosphere is the thin surface of the planet where life exists. This new, rapidly growing neurosphere is the electronic extension, the pulsing cyber repository of humanity's creative brainpower, its knowledge, history, culture, and increasingly commerce and entertainment. This is a global village vastly more comprehensive and interconnected than Marshall McLuhan could ever have envisioned when he coined the phrase more than 40 years ago.

This accelerating connectedness eliminates time and distance from hu-man communication, greatly contributing to the pervasive sense of speed in today's world, creating a transformational immediacy of human connect-edness. This connectivity in our society is approaching a singularity—the moment when an idea moves almost simultaneously through a population. This is something unimaginable until the last century. Distance meant time for information to move, which up until the 1800s was the speed of a horse going place to place. Compare that to today, just 200 years later, when communication is almost instantaneous.

A public and political example was the short yet furious furor in early 2006 over the Dubai Ports World deal. Just hours after news broke that the management of major American ports would be turned over to a Middle

Eastern company, public opinion, fueled and amplified by our electronic connectivity, swelled to the point where virtually every politician in the land was forced to condemn the deal. This took a little more than two weeks from beginning to end. As recently as 10 years ago, an issue like the Dubai Ports World deal took months to get debated. A newly connected populace came together in hours around an issue, took a position, and changed things.

Let's look at some data that shows this accelerating connectedness.

Cell Phones

In figure 13, which shows worldwide cell phone subscribers from 1990 and projected to 2025, notice that the steepest part of the curve starts during the last few years of the Threshold Decades, continues through the early years of the Shift Age, and does not start to level off until 2020. Applying this curve against global population projections, the point where 50 percent or more of the world has a cell phone occurs somewhere between 2012 and 2015. Imagine 50 percent of all people in the world, including the elderly and children in developed and less-developed countries, with instantaneous potential connectivity to each other. Nothing close to this immediate ability to personally communicate with others on such a global scale has ever existed before. We are fast approaching a historical shift.

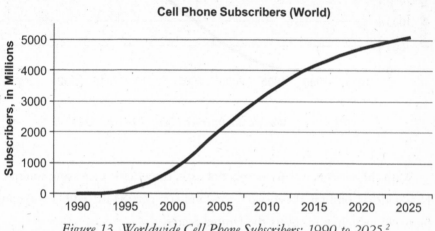

Figure 13. Worldwide Cell Phone Subscribers: 1990 to 2025.[2]

We must rely on imagination, not experience, when considering what this might mean and how it might feel.

The Internet

Figure 14 shows worldwide Internet users from 1985 and projected to 2025, and the sharp upward slope of the curve starts in the last five years of the Threshold Decades and only slows down around 2020. The phenomenal growth in Internet use that humanity has witnessed in the last 10 years is only the beginning. In terms of number of Internet users, we are only, as of this writing in late 2007, 50 percent of where we will be in some 15 years. Consider the transformation that the Internet has brought to your life and to society as a whole, and accept that as just the beginning. Again we must rely on imagination when thinking about the possibilities. There is no historical precedence for this amount of rich media interconnectivity.

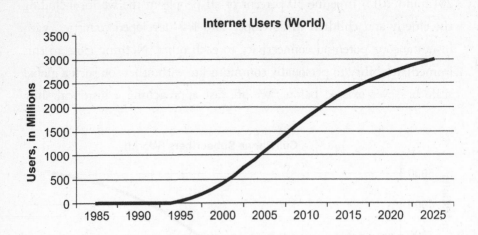

Figure 14. Worldwide Internet Users: 1985 to 2025.[3]

With this ever-increasing number of users comes ever-increasing Internet bandwidth. Combine these two forces, and you get the incredible curve in figure 15, which only covers the United States.

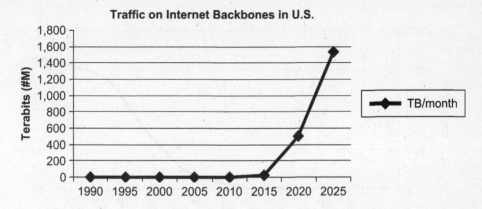

Figure 15. U.S. Traffic on Internet Backbones: 1990 to 2025.[4]

The rapid rise in Internet use and global bandwidth means we will see exponential growth in the amount of content available to those of us who are plugged in. Please note that figure 15 is only for the United States. It was difficult to find credible global projections that went out to 2025. The simple reason is that the growth of Internet traffic is so exponentially dynamic that it is hard to make an accurate prediction that far in the future. Cisco issued a report in 2006 that only projected out to 2011.[5] Their prediction was that global consumer use of the Internet would increase to a rate of 18 exabytes every month in 2011. That is 18 billion terabytes. The report went on to say that Internet traffic would quintuple between 2006 and 2011. Another way of stating this growth is that global Internet traffic will increase 86 times between 2000 and 2011. This growth is so rapid that it is impossible to project it out to 2025. The ever-increasing amount of video combined with the ongoing rapid increase in high-speed Internet connections is creating a connectedness that was practically unthinkable a decade ago. Once again we have to use our imagination rather than our experience as we hurtle toward this new connected global future.

Personal Computers

Finally, in figure 16, which shows computers in use around the world, we see the steepest part of the curve again starts during the last five years of

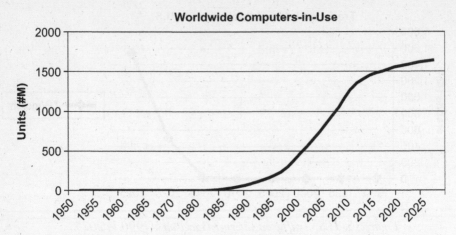

Figure 16. Worldwide Computers in Use: 1950 to 2025.[6]

the Threshold Decades and does not start to slow down until 2015. There is an earlier leveling off of computers than either cell phones or Internet use in part because computers are the oldest of the three technologies. Many of us have lived with computers for 20 years or more. Think how they have transformed just about every aspect of your life and have affected society. Now think about the fact that in terms of computers in use we are only at the halfway point on the path to where we will be in 2025.

To summarize, the accelerated global connectedness that began just before the start of the Shift Age will continue for the next 20 years. This connectedness and the exponential increase in links it provides will alter not just how we communicate but human society itself. This unstoppable force is one of the three forces of the Shift Age. It is the one that most people understand. Now let's look at the other two, which may be somewhat less obvious.

The Flow to Global

Overview

Humanity is heading toward a new global integration. We have moved through the geographical orientations of family, tribe, town, state, and country, and, due in part to our sheer numbers and our increasing electronic connectedness, we have arrived at the time of global orientation—a brand new place in our evolutionary history.

It is generally accepted that we are becoming a global economy. Historically, economics leads the way in change, followed by politics and culture. With the economic changes well underway and the social changes taking root, we are developing the identity of global citizens. The early part of the Shift Age will focus on integrating this new emerging sense of global citizenship with our past identities.

When the Eastern Bloc collapsed, first with the symbolic destruction of the Berlin Wall in 1989 and later with the disintegration of the Soviet Union in the early 1990s, the new global economy really began to take off. For the first time since the end of World War II, or one could argue since before World War I, there was a global economic playing field. As discussed in the prior chapter, this also allowed the beginning integration of East and West culturally, socially, and philosophically.

The simultaneous, historically unprecedented growth in electronic connectivity helped to accelerate this new flow to global. When the speed of communications accelerated, the world became smaller. Borders opened; boundaries collapsed; and economic transactions, culture, and world politics rushed in. Hundreds of millions of people for the first time were exposed to information and opportunity that were global in scope. There was a massive increase in migration, as workers from poorer countries went to richer countries to work for significantly higher wages that could be sent back home or used to fund the move of the entire family to a new land of opportunity.

As the world moved from the Threshold Decades, at the end of the Information Age, to the Shift Age, the final stage of human economic, social, and cultural evolution began. Humanity, over the last 10 millennia, moved from family to tribe to village to state to nation and has now appeared on the global stage. There is no turning back. One of the fundamental reasons for this shift is population growth—the sheer number of human beings alive on the planet. The flow to global is inevitable: the only border left for humanity is planetary.

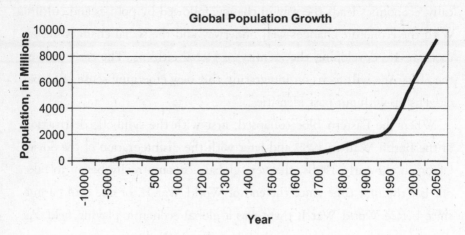

Figure 17. Global Population Growth.[7]

Figure 18 provides another way to look at population and the ages of humanity: it took modern humans approximately 150,000 years to reach a population of one billion. This roughly coincided with the end of the Agricultural Age. During the Industrial Age another three billion people were added, so that by 1974, at the beginning of the Information Age, there were four billion of us. There were roughly five billion at the start of the Threshold Decades and approximately six and a half billion at the dawn of the Shift Age.

Year (Estimated or Projected)	World Population	Years in Between
1804	1,000,000	
1927	2,000,000	123
1960	3,000,000	33
1974	4,000,000	14
1987	5,000,000	13
1999	6,000,000	12
2013	7,000,000	14
2028	8,000,000	15
2054	9,000,000	26

Figure 18. Milestones in World Population: When Did/Will We Reach the Next Billion.[8]

Economics First

The flow to global is first manifest in the emerging global economy. As this economic reorganization continues, there will be both opportunity and pain. The opportunity is still only partially apparent. There are larger markets for goods and services, lower-cost products, a freer flow of capital and information, and an incredible upswing in affluence and increased standard of living in such rapidly developing countries as China and India. The pain that countries feel does not mean that this flow to global is bad; it is part of the process of reorganization. As the great philosopher A. N. Whitehead wrote some 80 years ago, "[T]he major advances in civilization are processes which all but wreck the societies in which they occur...."[9]

Remember that one use of *threshold* we discussed relates to discomfort: pain threshold. The pain the United States felt in the past few years from the move of manufacturing jobs to lower-cost countries is a symptom of this new advance of civilization called the flow to global. It is part of an inevitable historical shift. Change can be painful. Structural reorganization can be painful. The move to automobiles 100 years ago was painful for companies that supplied the horse-and-buggy trade, but it was part of the transportation evolution. Cars were not necessarily bad; they were just the next step.

The conversation that is still taking place, usually in the political or manufacturing arenas, about whether the global economy is good or bad is irrelevant. The flow to global is not bad or good; it just is, and there is no turning back. The discussion should instead be about where the global economy is going and the optimal role to play in the global economy of the future. For the United States, I believe the future is to solidify and expand its role as the lead innovator and creator of intellectual property. Innovation has cascaded out of Silicon Valley and other high-tech areas around the country. When you include popular culture such as movies, video games, TV programs, books, and music recordings in the category, intellectual property is one of our most in-demand and financially powerful export products. Higher education in the United States attracts hundreds of thousands of foreign students a year because of its perceived value and stature. Intellectual property (IP) will become more important than hard assets for corporations and for countries in the Shift Age.

Currently there is a general disregard for patents and IP in China, Thailand, and other countries known for low-cost production. However, as these countries grow in economic clout and stature in the global economy, they will, of necessity, increasingly respect and honor IP. The United States needs to continue to press for the respect and legal protection of IP.

During the next 10 years, as China, the current king of the low-cost producers, becomes evermore affluent, due in large part to the infusion of foreign currency for its inexpensive goods, it will begin to price itself out of being low-cost. This will then provide the opportunity for other countries to move from poverty-driven, low-cost production to affluence to finally an economic nation of stature. This may well be the opportunity for the sub-Saharan countries to pull themselves up out of hunger and acute poverty. It is quite conceivable that by 2015 Africa will be the low-cost producer of goods for the rest of the world.

Culture and Politics

In human history, economics usually leads the way, followed by culture and politics. For example, America was "discovered" by Christopher Columbus because he was looking for a trade route to India (which is why Native Americans have been called Indians for centuries). So the desire for economic gain resulted in the European discovery of America. Once America was colonized, it started to develop its own culture and, with the American Revolution, its own politics. Empires initially are created for economic reasons. Politics and culture ensue.

The global economy, which is clearly forming, is the first step. Global culture and global politics will inevitably follow. This is the flow to global: a complete reorganization of humanity around the global concept. If you accept that the global economy is a fact and is here to stay, then you must also accept that global culture and global politics will follow, in their unique forms and shapes.

Due to the accelerating electronic connectedness, global culture is developing rapidly. Go to a store with a large selection of CDs (if you can still find one), and there will be a lot of shelf space for "World Music." That was not a category in music stores 10 years ago. User-generated content from around the world can be seen on Web sites such as YouTube. TV and radio signals from around the world can be consumed via the Internet. Culture will become less parochial and national in shape; it will become global in scope. To a great degree, it already is.

Politics and government are a bit harder to see because, at this stage in human evolution, government is the slowest moving part of society. It is the most bureaucratic, institutionalized, influenced by existing special interests, and filled with long-term workers or people who came to power because they are popular and have access to money. Today the government of almost any country moves more slowly than the entrepreneurs, corporations, and general public. Accelerating connectivity will force government to pick up the pace because it is more on display and can be lobbied more quickly. Still it sometimes feels as though our government leaders have become followers.

The flow to global is creating a world where the nation-state, that great invention of the Industrial Age, is an anachronism. A powerful nation-state with centralized power was necessary to aggregate smaller units of people into countries that provided identity, services, safety, education, and economic force. In the global age, nation-states are out of step, stuck in times past.

What will the new government be? The United Nations has performed its duty as best as possible throughout the Cold War and into the new millennium. It, however, is an organization comprised of nation-states, nation-states with their own agendas and political and economic alliances. Issues and crises tend to get addressed from the self-serving viewpoints of the nation-states.

Increasingly the major issues facing the citizens of the world are global. Global issues need global answers. Global warming is a primary example. There is absolutely no way any nation-state can solve this problem alone. The entire world needs to be involved in solving global warming, simply because it is a global problem. Global warming, as an issue, as a fact, as a problem to be addressed, will accelerate the movement toward the development of a global government. Issues like global warming, ocean restoration, allocation of natural resources such as water, space exploration, and the energy crisis will result in the creation of global agencies, empowered to coordinate efforts to address and solve problems.

I believe sometime in the next 10 years there will be the creation of a new global governing body that will be both an outgrowth of these global-issue-oriented organizations and something that will succeed the increasingly less relevant and gridlocked United Nations. It could perhaps evolve from that organization. The entity that I will call the Global Council could be charged with oversight of planetary issues, leaving the United Nations to manage and adjudicate political and economic disputes between nations. National governments will increasingly be left with the responsibilities for services, infrastructure, the safety of their citizens, and the maintenance of historical national heritage.

This Global Council will be created during the Shift Age. As all past economic and social entities such as towns, cities, counties, states, and nations created governmental structures in their own time, so the flow to global will necessitate the creation of this Global Council.

We are increasingly thinking of ourselves as global citizens.

The Flow to Individual

Overview

The changes that occurred during the Threshold Decades triggered the flow of power to the individual. The explosion of choice, the growth of free agency, the technologies and dynamics that moved us from hierarchies to networks, the ever-growing electronic connectedness and its increasing speed have all helped to migrate power from institutions to individuals. Gatekeepers are disappearing; disintermediation and its primary agent, the Internet, are reorganizing the economic landscape. The individual is becoming the primary economic unit, the micro-micro that is combining with the macro-macro of the flow to global. We are distinct individuals who are global citizens.

Free Agents with Choice and Control

The flow to individual can be traced to the movement from the Industrial Age through the Threshold Decades—from a production economy that was hierarchical to a knowledge- and information-based economy that is flat and networked. In the marketplace tens of millions of people have moved from being employees to being independent contractors. We have increasingly become a culture of free agents. We come together around projects or initiatives, do our work, and then move on to something else. Access to high-speed connectivity and to wireless technologies allows us to work anywhere. We can go to an office if we want to, but it is only necessary for in-person meetings and interactions.

In our personal lives this flow to individual is equally pronounced. We have become consumers of micro, not mass, media. We have completely customized media experiences. More than 100 million people walk around with iPods and other digital players, listening to their own personal sound track to life. We have our favorite Web sites bookmarked on our computers. We sit on the couch and use our remote controls to make second-to-second decisions about what to watch. We choose from hundreds of channels. We are in control. Those who program our televisions and, increasingly, online content are not.

The explosion of choice, described in the prior chapter, has firmly placed control and therefore power in our hands. We have come a long way from a century ago when Henry Ford, describing the Model T, said, "People can have any color they want, as long as it is black." We have come a long way from the 1970s, when in the United States the three broadcast networks were programmed by three people sitting in offices in Manhattan blocks apart from each other. The advent of the 24/7, "always on" culture means we can shop, work, and play whenever we want to, on our own schedules. We are in control. The remote control, the DVR, the downsizing of corporations, the growth of high-speed connectivity, the increase in all kinds of networks, be they work or social, and the explosion of choice in all areas allow us to completely customize our lives.

The End of Alienation?

Unlimited choice has also dealt a death blow to alienation. In the decades immediately after World War II, alienation was clearly present in the developed nations. Since there was only mass media, big business, and big government, if you were not in step with these big entities, you felt alienated. If you didn't fit in the popularly defined society, you felt left out. Now, in the Shift Age, alienation has largely disappeared because of unlimited choice. Our identities are aggregations of our choices. We determine what we like to listen to, watch, wear, or do for recreation; what we do for work and how and where we live is up to us. We no longer measure ourselves against the mass models. Instead we group ourselves around our interests and activities. Everything is possible.

The Micro-Micro

How will the flow to individual change the world? I believe there will be a decrease in the power of institutions and organizations. Society is being reorganized around the macro-macro, or the flow to global, and the micro-micro, the flow to individual. The smallest and largest economic units have increasing gravitational pull. The institutions that came into existence over the last 300 years are declining in power, membership, and influence. Residual social institutions from the days of landed aristocracy or from the gilded age of robber barons are declining in importance. Unions, service organizations, and the corporation itself, while all still important, are no longer as much a part of one's identity as in generations past. What one does is more important than who one works for.

The mass market is in decline as an influence. We deal now with an aggregation of small, targeted, micro markets. The "Long Tail" concept Chris Anderson so excellently described in his book of the same name is the new shape of the market in the digital world.[10] Now that products are as much digital as physical, markets will and can be smaller and evermore customized. The word *fragmentation* has been used a lot in recent years. It is an old reference point as it speaks to the fragmentation of the marketplace, which assumes a mass market. Think instead of the recent phenomena in the move from mass to micro as a historical process.

Individuals define themselves by the decisions they make as much as by the group to which they belong. This will accelerate as the explosion of choice, customization, and flexibility allows individuals to be individuals and to choose their own paths, even if in small ways.

The flow to global and the flow to individual are combining to reshape how we think of ourselves. Increasingly we are self-articulating individuals who identify as global citizens. The concern we have for issues such as global warming drives us to first think of ourselves as global citizens and then to develop a global conscience.

Conclusion

THREE FORCES DOMINATE the Shift Age:

- Accelerating electronic connectedness
- The flow to global
- The flow to individual

If you reflect on your personal experience and observe the world stage carefully, you will see these forces at play. All three are laying the foundation for a shift in consciousness that will occur during the next 20 to 30 years. This new consciousness could well be a new dawn in humanity's evolutionary journey, the probable coming of an evolution shift, the Shift Age defined by consciousness.

But, but, there are rough times ahead. Change is rapid; problems are massing and will force us to solve them. Global warming, religious fundamentalism, alternative and renewable energy, excessive worldwide debt, overpopulation and the poverty it creates, and shortages of vital resources as basic as clean water are all major issues we must face. Everything is shifting. The old ideas don't work—and they shouldn't because they are from the past—and the problems rushing at us are in the present and coming from the future. The three forces of the Shift Age are changing human society every minute of every day.

During the Threshold Decades we crossed from what was into what will be. The Shift Age is the time when we must not look backward for solutions, for the door to that room has closed. We stand on shifting ground. We need to live in the present to succeed in shaping a golden future. And there is a golden future ahead of us, if we navigate the next 10 years with vision, the ability to adapt, and a willingness to embrace change.

For those of you who look around and despair, remember that line, "The darkest hour is just before dawn." If we can get to that dawn, the Shift Age will become one of the most important, most significant times in the history of modern man.

PART II:
COMMENTARY ON THE SHIFT AGE

INTRODUCTION

The future, what's that?

—Belisario, a member of the Nukak-Maku tribe who left the
Columbian jungle to join the modern world in 2006

IN THE PUREST sense of time, there is only the present moment. Life is a constant stream of present moments. The past is our collective memory, and the future our collective dreams, aspirations, and fears. That being said, the future does show up unevenly in our present—and now at an accelerating rate. The columns that follow offer perspective on changes you might feel personally and on the global direction our collective present moments might take.

Part II of this book is comprised of columns taken from the Evolution Shift blog at http://www.evolutionshift.com. A "best of the blog" selection, the columns have been grouped by subject and have been edited for book publication. Links, an essential characteristic of blogs, have been removed. In each chapter, the columns are organized chronologically as they were published online.

Part I of this book introduces you to the historical context and dynamics of the Shift Age. Part II is front-line reporting and commentary on this age as it begins. You certainly don't need to read the chapters in order. Start with whatever subject most interests you. It is recommended that you do read each chapter chronologically, as the columns have been edited with that sequence in mind. This part of the book is structured to be read easily in the midst of a hectic life.

CHAPTER 4:
GOING GLOBAL

T HE GLOBALIZATION OF almost everything, from economics to politics to culture, is undeniable; it—along with electronic connectedness and the influence of the individual—distinguishes the current stage in our evolution, the Shift Age.

Because economics is often the trailblazer, pioneering new lines of thought and putting them into action, "Exit Greenspan, the Economist's Rock Star," "It Is All Global," and "Debt, Credit, Obligations, and Trust" focus on financial matters. "The World Cup Points the Way" shows us how culture is following economics down a macro path. In "Made in China," one country's rapid development is emblematic of the speed of change that characterizes our lives. And, finally, "Damaged Brands" looks at how worldwide opinion can be won or lost overnight in today's electronic environment.

Exit Greenspan, the Economist's Rock Star

February 4, 2006

This past week Alan Greenspan stepped down after 18 years as chairman of the Federal Reserve. This was not only a story that was on the front page of the business sections of the newspapers; it was on the front page of the newspapers and one of the lead stories on the nightly newscasts. The Great Greenspan had steered the country through crises and was now riding off into his emeritus sunset, a true economic hero.

I believe that Greenspan was the last, great Fed chairman in the traditional mold. The definition of success has changed. Ben Bernanke and those who will follow him face a new dynamic that will measure effectiveness in the job: their success in global cooperation as it effects monetary supply and other Fed instruments.

This first popped into my mind during the run-up in short-term interest rates that Greenspan led in the last three years. When the constant quarter-point raises in the Fed rate were under way, the consensus, based on history, was that, after a lag time, the long-term interest rates would also rise. The primary focus was the mortgage market, as historically those rates went up.

Something happened: they didn't really move up that much. What was going on? Greenspan himself was surprised. When he couldn't put the skids on the heated housing market by waving the raising-interest-rate wand, he started to sputter about the "housing bubble" in a way similar to his "frothy exuberance" for the stock market in the 1990s. The Fed didn't seem to affect the mortgage market much, people were flipping houses, and Greenspan was on the sidelines with a certain sense of moral indignation.

My instinctive reaction was that there was some macro reason for this, some dynamic flowing from the fact that the global economy has taken root. This point of view was heightened when looking at the general slow, spotty post-recession recovery. Economists couldn't quite put their fingers on it. Was it a rolling recovery, moving through the economy sector by sector? Was it a service industry recovery with a dark manufacturing problem at its core? A general wringing of economists' hands, as the Fed, under the tall shadow of Greenspan, no longer seemed astride the horse of recovery and managed interest rates.

Well, lo and behold, what emerged? All that money the United States was shipping over to China bundled up in record trade deficits was being reinvested in interest-bearing investments in the United States. The Chinese were taking our money and offering it back to us as mortgage loans, to such a great degree that the supply of their money more than kept pace with the heated housing demand.

The global economy has irrevocably taken root; there is no turning back; global is a dynamic flow that is rearranging all nation-state economies. What does this mean? It means that Greenspan is the last Fed chairman to preside over and adjust the economic levers of the United States as a nation-state economy. His tenure basically was contemporary with the birth and growth of the global economy in the Information Age.

So what lies ahead for Bernanke? The specifics are certainly not known at this time, but he is the first Fed chairman whose tenure started with the new global economy in place. What that means in terms of the Fed's operational tactics remains to be seen. What it means in the largest sense is that the definition of success for Bernanke and all his successors will forever, in part, be how they incorporate the dynamic flow to global and the global economy in what they do and how they analyze the metrics they look at.

The news coverage of the transfer of power from the rock star Greenspan to the rhythm guitarist Bernanke played on the hard-act-to-follow theme. As in, "Poor Ben, he has to follow a living legend." Well, that is in fact true, but what B.B. now has is a chance to define "Outstanding Performance by a Fed Chairman" with a new songbook, written and performed on the global stage.

• • •

The World Cup Points the Way

July 17, 2006

All the yellow cards, red cards, fake injuries, and head butts aside, the recently completed World Cup was a magnificent global phenomenon. The world came together around the single biggest sporting event on earth. It has always been the quadrennial big event, but this time there was a certain amplification that was different.

In the four years since the 2002 World Cup, there has been a growing recognition that we are all part of a global economy. Thomas L. Friedman's *The World is Flat* came out in 2005. Every day there seems to be a story about India or China and their exploding economies, how these economies are linking up with the United States and other countries, and how these and other economies with their growth have put upward pressure on the price of energy and most commodities. Certainly in the United States—and I would venture to say in most countries—there is more of a sense of being a global citizen than in 2002. Since then, there have been tens, if not hundreds, of millions of new high-speed Internet connections to homes and businesses, and the number of people using wireless devices with Internet connectivity and video around the world has soared. All this made the 2006 World Cup more of an inclusive and readily available event than ever before.

The second thing to point out is that in the United States the ratings soared over those in 2002. Most of this increase was due to the fact that the Cup was in Germany and not Korea or Japan, and therefore the game times were better for U.S. viewing. Nevertheless, Americans watched in record number, despite the less than stellar performance by the American team. I was in an airport a couple of times when games were on, and people crowded in front of the TVs in bars and restaurants, watching matches, with enthusiasm previously reserved for NFL play-offs or the World Series. This time, the World Cup resonated with Americans, who seemed to be more than curious about this sport of soccer that everyone else calls football.

What really hit home for me is that more than 300 million people watched the World Cup final between France and Italy live. Think about that: there were that many people doing the exact same thing, watching the same game, all at the same time. That is more people than the population of the United States right now. That audience is more than three times the worldwide audience of the Super Bowl. It was also estimated that the live audience plus all the people who didn't watch the game but saw highlights in the 24 hours after the game added up to almost one billion viewers. Even assuming duplication, that is a staggering number.

We are moving toward a much more global society than exists today. We are all starting to think of ourselves as global citizens. We have all understood that we now live in a global economy, where something that happens in one part of the world affects the economies of countries all over the world. The Internet, communications satellites, live TV, and billions of cell phones around the world have created a world where, in terms of communication, there is no longer any time and distance. When everything travels at the speed of light and everything is always available, there is no sense of distance or time. Communicating via the Internet or via a wireless device with someone 10,000 miles away takes the same time as communicating with someone 10,000 feet or 10,000 inches away. So technology and communications are the first step. This first step has enabled us to gather around, log on, or push a button so we can all watch a game in Berlin live.

Communications are global, the economy is becoming global, and history teaches us that culture and politics follow economics. So we are, to a significant degree, moving toward a global culture. The World Cup points the way.

• • •

Made in China

July 23, 2007

Fifteen years ago, when Americans went shopping and came across the phrase "made in China," it usually was on small, inexpensive trinkets, toys, and souvenirs. Ten years ago we started to see these words on apparel. Five years ago we started to see these words everywhere. During the last five months, if we saw these words, it might have meant the death of our pets, food-borne illness, or perhaps poisoning.

The Chinese government is taking this quality issue very seriously as billions of dollars of exports are put at risk. Doing what they have historically done, the Chinese executed the former government official who had been the head of the State Food and Drug Administration for taking bribes and looking the other way on safety and production issues. In the last week they also closed the companies that shipped poisonous products overseas. We certainly need to hold the Chinese accountable for any and all defective and life-threatening products that make it to the United States. The historical levels of government oversight in the production of goods, be it labor conditions or product quality, are much lower in China—and many other developing countries—than in the United States.

The larger context in which this issue must be viewed is that China is going through a process that has never occurred with any country in history, at least with any major international power. China is going from being a basically agricultural society to becoming both an industrial and informational powerhouse. The Agricultural Age started 10,000 years ago, the Industrial Age started 300 years ago, and the Information Age started 30 years ago. China is collapsing a 300-year-long cultural transition into 25 years. In 1975, China was an insular, agrarian society with a third-world economy. Now China is one of the most economically dominant countries in the world. The Chinese are dealing with issues and new situations in years that most other countries took decades to pass through. No wonder there is horrendous pollution and environmental degradation, slave labor, unhealthy products, and abject poverty coupled with incredible wealth. It is going to take some years to bring a level of stability and government oversight to this exploding economy.

While doing research on the historical trends of trademarks and patents, three things jumped out at me regarding China.[1] First, in 1975 China was not even on the radar in the number of patents issued in the country. In 2000 some 13,000 were issued; in 2005 more than 53,000. (By comparison, the U.S. numbers were 144,000 and 157,000 in 2000 and 2005, respectively.) This puts China in fourth place after the United States, Japan, and South Korea—and it's moving up fast.

Second, in terms of trademarks, which are related more to business creation than intellectual property creation, the numbers are nothing less than amazing. In 1975 China was not on the list of the top countries. By 2000 China was the number one country with 151,000, and in 2005 the number of trademarks had jumped to 260,000. By comparison the numbers for the United States were 109,000 in 2000 and 132,000 in 2005, in both cases second place.

Third, after the United States, China is now the second largest manufacturer. In 1975 the Chinese were fifth in the world. An interesting historical footnote that completely surprised me is that in 1750 and again in 1800 China was the number one manufacturing country in the world. Since this was before the Industrial Age took root, these numbers largely reflect agricultural production and trade. In 1850 China was tied with the United Kingdom for first place. Of course, from 1900 through 2006, the United States is far and away number one, with a 45 percent share of all global manufacturing in 1950 and 29 percent in 2006. Predictions are that in 2015 China will surpass the United States when both countries will each be responsible for about 20 percent of the global manufacturing output. What was old is soon to be new.

There is another way to compare the United States and China. In the United States, it was basically in the time from the Civil War to World War I that the country fully moved from being an agricultural society to an industrial one. (After all, it was the industrial North that defeated the agricultural South in the Civil War.) That was a span of 50 years. During that time, all the oversight and legislation regarding production began to be put in place, thanks in large part to the muckrakers and their campaigns. China is going through this same process in less than 25 years while at the same time integrating the new information economy. This means that the governmental oversight of this exploding production engine of a country will constantly struggle to keep up.

Yes, China is going to be one of the most dominant economic powers in the decades ahead. We all know that. It is how the Chinese manage this historically unparalleled speed and magnitude of growth that will determine if "made in China" becomes a respected and valued brand.

• • •

It Is All Global

August 16, 2007

I view the recent upheavals in the financial markets through two future-thinking filters. The first is that we are moving to a new and developing global society and that this can be seen economically. The second is that debt is something that must be looked at with new perspective. Today we look at the first filter.

Humanity has conclusively moved into the global stage of its evolution. There is no turning back. There are more than six billion of us, and that fact alone is enough to reorganize human endeavor to a global orientation. Human history shows us that economics usually leads the way with politics and culture following close behind. Columbus "discovered" America because he was looking for a trade route to India (at least now we call our indigenous people Native Americans, no longer Indians) for the economic gain of Europe. American politics and culture ultimately followed this initially economically driven endeavor.

BNP Paribas, the largest publicly traded bank in France, suspended investors' ability to withdraw money from funds that had invested in American mortgage securities. When one of the largest financial institutions in Europe shuts down trading because of rising foreclosures in California, it is clear the financial marketplace is global. Of course, we have known this for years, particularly since the advent of electronic fund transfers. Money flows electronically around the world without any regard for borders or time zones. Now that money has lost much of its physical characteristic, it is much more mutable and moves freely and quickly from one investment vehicle or financial institution to another, literally at the speed of light due to fiber optics.

I've argued that the Fed and its chairman can no longer look at the United States as a stand-alone financial marketplace, where pulling this lever and pushing that button predictably make the desired economic adjustments. The global economic marketplace has become way too connected and interrelated to continue with that thinking. A panic in one country affects the stock market in another country. Thousands of first-time home buyers walking away from houses they purchased with exotic sub-prime mortgages in the suburban valleys of California brings paralysis and illiquidity to a trading desk in Paris.

We are now seeing market conditions that have not existed before. Hedge funds can move money electronically so quickly across multiple markets that they no longer behave as they did in the past. The U.S. stock markets are experiencing volatility due in part to this factor. These hedge funds use quantitative computer trading programs based on incredibly extensive historical data. The funds have been unable to liquidate their holdings in mortgage-backed securities, so they raise cash by selling equities in the liquid stock markets. The numbers are so large that they then trigger the computer buy/sell programs. Since these are somewhat similar from fund to fund, there are huge amounts of simultaneous transactions, which drive markets up or down in minutes. Everyone is scrambling to keep abreast of the current crisis using tools based on outdated historical data.

Metaphysicians and Eastern spiritual leaders have long spoken about how everything is one, how all is interconnected. They speak of how an occurrence in one part of the world causes a reaction in another part of the world, how everything is an interconnected web. This view has no room for national or political boundaries. Well, if first-time homeowners in a California valley make the tough decision to walk away from their home and their mortgage and that decision affects a debt trader in Paris, is it not the same vision?

The weaving together of the new and emerging global financial market is dynamic and ongoing. I sense that we will look back to this time in the financial markets as a generally recognized signpost pointing us down the road of an increasingly integrated global human society.

· · ·

Debt, Credit, Obligations, and Trust

August 20, 2007

It feels like we are moving through a watershed moment in both the U.S. and global financial markets. When the mortgage securities market collapses as though it was the tulip bulb market centuries ago in Holland, it is truly time to pause and look at what has been allowed to occur. Mortgages, secured by real estate, have long been considered a secure investment, unlike, say, junk bonds. Now the marketplace is saying that it cannot value them, so no one is either buying them or allowing them to be used as loan collateral. Wow!

In the new global electronic trading marketplace, a vast number of new investment vehicles have been created in the past 20 years. These new investment products, evermore sophisticated and varied, gave investors additional ways to hedge portfolios—take on or alleviate risk—and accelerated the electronic flow of capital around the world. They also were created, in part, by investment banks to provide new sources of fee revenue. This was the beginning of the problem; it led investment instruments to become disconnected from the underlying asset. Once a mortgage was granted to a home buyer, that same mortgage was pooled into a mortgage-backed security and sold to a buyer, often in a matter of weeks or months. There was no longer any connection between the homeowner, who was paying down the mortgage, and the holder of the mortgage. No relationship existed. As we all know, having a relationship can stabilize any situation.

I remember buying my first home. I went through a detailed and rigorous application process to obtain the mortgage, and then I mailed my mortgage passbook into the savings and loan association every month with my payment. Days later I received it back in the mail with the latest payment credited against interest and the reduction in principal. I was one of those risky loans as I had put only 10 percent down. During the entire four years I owned that home I did this month in and month out. This type of relationship has ceased to exist. The days of the Bailey S&L from *It's a Wonderful Life* are long gone.

In January, I predicted that the residential real estate marketplace would not recover this year. Not only is that prediction on track, but the current market meltdown in mortgage-backed securities has extended the length of the downturn significantly. It will not be until the second half of 2008, at the earliest, that the national real estate marketplace has a chance to make a consolidated move upward again.

Whenever I look ahead to the 2008 elections and the four or five years beyond them, one of the most troubling areas is debt. It is at record levels and increasing. Consumer debt to maintain lifestyles, corporate borrowing, mortgage debt, and, of course, the more than $50 trillion of obligations the U.S. government is carrying continue to spiral, taking on a life of their own. The issue here is the disconnect with economic fundamentals. There is no historical precedent. Investment has become speculation, across the board. People buy homes with no money down and no payment of principal and with a promise to pay higher rates. Companies borrow at historically low rates, betting on a significant increase in revenues. The worst culprit is the U.S. government, as no one in it can tell you how the funds borrowed today will be paid back tomorrow.

Everyone is borrowing against a future event: housing prices always going up, sales increasing on plan, and the U.S. government elevating Alfred E. Neumann as their financial guru with his philosophy of "What? Me worry?"

Hedge funds, and the major investment banks that service them, are to some degree at fault in this current downturn, as they speculated on investment vehicles that were disconnected from underlying assets, used credit to leverage themselves even further, and then, when faced with illiquidity (how could they not see that coming?), dumped equities to cover as best they could. During the course of the next several months, we are going to see some hedge funds collapse, others sell their remaining holdings for a discount to other funds, and a continuing crisis in the mortgage and mortgage security marketplaces. The stock market could in fact resume its path to new records, but that will not solve these problems.

The real question, and the one that has the most dangerous possible ramifications, is to what degree has trust evaporated and for how long? Since World War II, investment instruments created in the United States have been looked on as safe and secure. In a troubled world, investment capital has flowed to the United States as a trusted and safe place. This is now called into question. Those who invest vast amounts of money around the world are now going to ask for more accountability and security for any investment vehicles created and based in the United States. This country is going to have to be accountable to others in this growing global economy in new ways.

We have all, to some degree, felt the pain of being speculators. Speculation is not to be trusted in the near term. Will our credit markets, debt instruments, and the great names in the investment community maintain our trust going forward? I hope so for all of us.

• • •

Damaged Brands

September 4, 2007

The past few weeks have not been good ones for products manufactured in China and financial instruments created in the United States. The "made in China" brand is now untrustworthy to millions of American consumers. New, mortgage-backed debt instruments, highly valued by U.S. bond rating agencies, are now questioned in financial capitals around the world.

In an earlier column entitled "Made in China," I discussed certain historical forces and timelines that, to some degree, are causing the recent rash of dangerous products from China. In a historically short period of 25 years, the country is moving from being a rural, agrarian economy to one of the largest industrial economies in the world. In addition, in this same time period, it is moving from being a secretive, xenophobic, communist state run by a central planning committee to a major player on the world economic stage with standards of safety and openness. This huge a transition in such a short time has never occurred, so a number of sizable bumps in the road are to be expected.

This historical perspective notwithstanding, the "made in China" brand is in serious trouble. Odds are, you, the reader, are either a parent or a pet owner. If you are a parent, particularly of a young child, you now look at toy packaging and think twice before you buy a toy that has the words "made in China" printed on it. Lead poisoning? Not in my household! Magnets that can be easily swallowed? Not for my child! If you are a pet owner, you also think twice about buying pet food with those same words. Hundreds if not thousands of pets worldwide have been poisoned by "made in China" pet food, so why take the risk?

To some degree the American consumer has brought this on herself. In the search for ever-lower prices, she has embraced things made in third-world countries because they cost less. This downward pressure on prices makes all companies producing goods in China, American or not, relentless in finding cheaper ways to produce. What was assumed was that safety would be respected as it is elsewhere in the world. Obviously, this is not the case. When the safety and, in fact, the life of a child or a pet may be in question, the value of lower prices goes out the window. So now, to some degree, "made in China" means potentially unsafe goods.

Since the end of World War II, the United States has been the dominant economy in the world. The dollar has been the dominant currency, and the U.S. financial markets and investment instruments have been considered blue-chip and trustworthy. When the investment banks and rating services of Wall Street team up to offer the world highly rated investment products, they have been perceived globally as legitimate, secure, and more or less liquid. This reputation is being tested with the ongoing problems in the mortgage-backed securities marketplace. There have been unexpected illiquidity and questionable underlying value, which have caused havoc elsewhere in the financial landscape.

This provoked an outcry in the financial capitals of the world for more involvement in the U.S. investment marketplace.

In the past 20 years, all kinds of new investment instruments have been created by Wall Street investment banks in their ongoing quest for more and more fee income. So far, the global marketplace has embraced this process. The banks and rating services got bigger, and global investors gladly bought new financial products as they came from the top investment brand in the world, Wall Street. Now the global marketplace is demanding a place at the table when these instruments get created and rated. The Wall Street investment brand has been damaged.

These two damaged brands point to the ongoing move to a global society. China must embrace the openness, safety, and accountability in the manufacturing process that other countries expect or risk serious economic consequence. U.S. financial institutions and markets must open up to more high-level involvement from around the world or face a much tougher sales environment in the future. We are in a global economy, and we are moving toward a more global culture. This is nothing less than a transformation, and any transformation can cause pain and discomfort.

CHAPTER 5:
TECHNOLOGY AND TRANSFORMATION

T HE WILD CHANGE that is emblematic of the Shift Age is perhaps most visible in the technology that drives our accelerating electronic connectedness. Personal computers, cell phones, and the Internet, essentially unknown 30 years ago, permeate our lives today. Technology has forever changed—and continues to change—how we act and interact. Innovation after innovation blurs reality and virtuality, work and play, public and personal.

This chapter looks at technology; its evolution toward cheaper, faster, smaller, easier, more portable, more powerful, and more intuitive; and its impact on us individually and collectively.

Sometimes It Is Easy to See the Future: A Futuristic Pocketful

July 5, 2006

Across the full spectrum of human endeavor, it is often hard to see what the future might be. Trend lines can be seen, and directions understood, but specific pictures of the future can be vague. However, our future shows up most clearly in the area of technology. Technology lets us see new potential. It shows us new tools that may or may not become universally useful and provides us with possibilities to expect.

There were a couple of news items recently about technology that gave me a clear view of living in the future. The first was about a new flash drive, and the second about microchip research.

In the past year or two, portable flash drives have become ubiquitous. The flash drive is one of those tech items that make life easier and change behavior. When going to a client's office for a presentation, taking work home from the office, or just choosing to travel light, flash drives free us from toting laptops or burning DVDs. Just drag the presentation or work to the flash drive, put it in your pocket, and away you go. Initially the drives offered 64 and 128 megabytes of storage, but you can now routinely buy a gigabyte for the same price. I predict that in the next two years flash drives will be available for less than $25 that will have five gigabytes of storage. This will mean we can carry more storage in our pocket than was in an average desktop 20 years ago or a laptop 10 years ago.

The news that made me see the future was about the flash drives coming on the market this month. In addition to storage, these new flash drives also have basic software functionality, so, in a sense, you can travel with a portable computer in your pocket. Lexar, one of the leading companies in the flash drive business, is coming out with a product called PowerToGo that licenses something called Creedo Personal. This enables the flash drive to become a "portable Windows XP ecosystem," according to Lexar. Available with one or two gigs of storage, this new type of flash drive allows you to carry your documents and a mini operating system wherever you go. It replicates the Windows Start menu and browser. This means that, for simple work, you no longer need a computer when mobile. It is hard to find a home, office, or hotel that does not have a computer. Just find a computer, plug in your flash drive with its own software, and operate securely, without upsetting anything on the host computer and without leaving a trace.

The future is obvious. There are computers everywhere, and we all travel with our own personalized flash drive/storage device in our pocket. If airlines can put flat screen TVs in plane seats, they can put in basic computers with pop-out keyboards. Hotels can supply connected keyboards to rooms that have portals for flash drives. I can just hear road warriors in the year 2010 marveling at the guy in seat 10C who is still carrying a laptop. Gee, remember when we thought a laptop was the end-all in mobile computing?

The other news addresses the ever-increasing speed and power of computing technology. First, grant me a minor digression. Moore's Law (computing power doubles every 18 months and is reduced in cost by half during the same time) has recently been questioned as perhaps a formula that has run its cycle, given all the speed and power breakthroughs of the last decade. Maybe we have maxed out speed, power, and price in computing, and increases in power and speed will become incremental.

Well, I guess not. Researchers at IBM and the Georgia Institute of Technology announced last month they broke the speed record for silicon-based chips with a semiconductor that could operate 250 times faster than chips currently in use today. Not 5 times or 10 times, but 250 times! It will take years for this chip to make its way into all our cool tech gadgets, but this means that a lot of other things will happen between now and then. Slower chips will cost less, bigger chips will cost less, chips will become lighter and smaller, and software creators in all fields will see new possibilities to create things given new opportunities for processing speed. It is one of those amazing tech breakthroughs that will allow other amazing things to occur.

The flash drives and electronic calculators of 2008 will be more powerful and faster and will have more storage than the biggest mainframe computer in the United States had 50 years before. Now that is a futuristic pocketful!

• • •

Happy Birthday, PC!

August 21, 2006

It was 25 years ago this month that the personal computer was born. In August 1981 IBM launched the PC. This was five years after Steve Jobs and Steve Wozniak came out with the Apple 1, but it was the IBM PC and its rapid acceptance first in the corporate world and then in homes that ushered in the explosive growth of personal computing. The importance of the introduction of the PC cannot be overstated from the vantage point of 2006.

Prior to 1981 computing basically was mainframe computing. Corporations and universities had air-conditioned rooms housing large computers that were operated by computer operators and run by computer programmers and systems analysts. Do you know someone who currently works as a computer operator? Now we're all computer operators: e-mailing, surfing, working, creating.

The innovation that Apple brought to the computing industry was first embraced by geeks and computer hobbyists, but it showed the way to desktop computing. When IBM launched its PC, it targeted its corporate user base with the IBM 5150 launched on August 12, 1981. The model had 16 kilobytes of memory—yes, kilobytes. It used cassette tapes and floppy disks to load and save data: seen any of those at a garage sale recently? The last time I saw a floppy disk it was being used as a coaster.

IBM had tried to sell PCs before 1981, but they were too expensive for what they delivered. Once IBM launched the 5150, it had a price tag under $1,600 (roughly $4,000 today, adjusted for inflation). With constant upgrades in memory and speed, sales took off. Every office got at least one, and someone was trained to run it. During the late 1980s and early 1990s the IBM PCs started to land on the majority of desktops in corporations. At this same time the early adopters started to buy them—and Apples—for home use.

In 1981 IBM, having owned the mainframe business, thought the future was in computing hardware, so it outsourced software to Microsoft and chips to Intel. Hmmmmmm! At the time, a young Bill Gates stated that the future of computing would be in software. Regardless of what you may think of Gates and Microsoft, that statement was one of the most accurate and monumental business predictions of all time. Jobs was the visionary who saw the possibility of personal computing. Gates was the visionary who saw the possibility of world domination by putting a computer on every desktop.

Today there are slightly more than 70 PCs for every 100 people in the United States. Not only are PCs ubiquitous, they are infinitely faster and more powerful than what IBM sold 25 years ago. The laptop I am writing on is more powerful than pre-PC mainframes that took teams of people to run. I am always amazed by that now-clichéd statement that I have more computing power at my fingertips than was on the Apollo spacecraft that went to the moon.

When the vast number of computers in the world is multiplied by the power and speed of recent generations of computers and that is multiplied by the Internet and then again by high-speed Internet, we arrive at the incredible cyberspace we live in today. When the rapid market growth of intelligent phones and wireless devices that access the Internet and e-mail is layered on top, we have a level of connectivity that has never existed before and would have been hard to imagine even 30 years ago, except by science fiction writers.

It is this platform, this connectivity, this simultaneity, this power, this access that excites me and gives me great hope for our collective future. For centuries, humanity's existence, progress, and evolution have, to a great degree, been limited by distance, lack of awareness of other cultures, lack of shared knowledge, and the time it took to communicate.

Yes, there were the telephone, the radio, and the television, but it was the PC and the explosive growth it experienced in the last 25 years combined with broadband that brought power to the individual, disintermediation to the marketplace, and unimagined connectivity to humanity.

Happy birthday, PC!

. . .

Sometimes It Is Easy to See the Future: Head to the Beach for a Day at Work

September 12, 2006

I'm attracted to the "new," and I consume a lot of media, so I often read about things that, when combined with another news or product story, point to a clear trend or possibility.

In the past decade the price for computer hard drive storage dropped precipitously. Then came flash drives that also dropped dramatically in price in the past couple of years. You can now buy a flash drive with a gigabyte of memory for less than the price of 256 megabytes two years ago. The other dynamic is the miniaturization of memory: memory that fits in your shirt pocket.

There was a recent mention in the press about a new line of Sony USB drives that take this to the next stage. The Micro Vault Tiny USB drives are approximately an inch long and half an inch wide with the thickness of a quarter. They use a compression technology called Virtual Expander that allows up to three times as much data as usual to be put on the device. The storage range is from 256 megabytes to 4 gigabytes. Just think about that for a minute: more storage in a flash drive the size of a quarter than was in the average laptop 10 years ago.

I write a lot, and I don't always want to lug around a laptop, even an ultra-light one, so flash drives are a wonderful thing. I always carry one with the contents of my blog, posts I'm working on, the book I'm writing, everything on the flash drive. Most places I go there is a computer available. So, if I have downtime at a client site, stay with a friend, or make a quick trip without a laptop and stay at a hotel, I can always plug in the flash drive and continue to work.

Another recent development is the increasing storage capacity and miniaturization of external hard drives. You can now buy one with 60 to 100 gigabytes that is the size of a small paperback book. This makes it easy to back up files, and it means that you can have stripped-down computers at work and at home or in your second home and carry a small hard drive back and forth. As stripped-down laptops come on the market in the years ahead, buy a $200 laptop, a $50 flash drive, and a $75 external hard drive, and you have cheap and very portable computing. Combine that with another coming development and a video camera, and you can broadcast live from anywhere.

That coming development is the Sprint Nextel commitment to a 4G wireless network, which will combine broadband Internet access with wireless communications. Using a technology called WiMax, this network will allow for mobile videoconferencing, live video feeds without the cost of satellite time, and connecting to practically anything live, online, with a device in your hand. Amazing!

Think about progressions. Videoconferencing started out in the 1980s when communications companies set up studios in different cities that had uplink capability. In each city, employees went to a studio for a scheduled, expensive interaction, usually one-way with top management. The next step was having downlinks into each corporate office, so employees didn't need to leave the office. Then came the camera embedded in a laptop, which connected to the Internet, allowing basic videoconferencing, as long as you're plugged in and online. With 4G, you can videoconference with anyone from anywhere at anytime. Talk about disintermediation!

Think about the current poster child for disintermediation in the world of video: YouTube. With 4G, it could offer what it does now—videos made in the past—along with a section of live streams from around the world. Hey, it's that Evolution Shift futurist guy live from the beach or that real estate TV mogul live from Albuquerque. Live streaming from anywhere to everywhere. Everyone is a network: one-to-many and one-to-one telecasting. All the possibilities of broadband combined with mobility.

Sprint Nextel's partners in the 4G effort are Motorola for equipment, Samsung for network infrastructure, and Intel for chips. I mention this because the 3G effort to date has been underwhelming. But this combination of four companies at the top of their respective markets is one that will not stand down from this wonderful vision.

So put your memory in your shirt pocket, put your wireless device with video camera in your shorts pocket, and head for the beach, mountaintop, or backyard for a live interactive day at the office with your colleagues. Not a bad solution to the near future when gas is $7 a gallon and business travel is often too expensive to undertake.

• • •

Always Faster

September 20, 2006

Just when you thought you had caught up with the latest technology, along comes another breakthrough to make you feel unnerved by the speed of change. This week the stunning announcement of a breakthrough in chip technology turned my head. As I read the news, the thought balloon over my head would have been a big "WOW!!" had I been in a comic strip.

Researchers from Intel and the University of California, Santa Barbara announced they created a silicon-based chip that can produce laser beams. This means that it will be possible to use laser light rather than wires to send data between chips. For the first time, researchers were able to bond a silicon chip with a wafer that emits light when electricity is applied. This means information will move 100 times faster at a fraction of the cost. In the past few years there has been speculation that Moore's Law (computing power doubles every 18 months and also drops by half in cost), which has driven the growth of computing over the past few decades, is finally coming up against limitations of physics. Well, this answers that question!

Lasers have been used to transmit vast amounts of data via fiber optic cables over long distances, but the speed of data transmission between chips in the computer has been much slower. With this breakthrough, computer engineers will be able to rethink and reconfigure computer construction, resulting in significantly faster computers. This reminds me of the generally accepted fact regarding jet fighter planes over the past 20 years: that the pilot is the weak link in the complex computerized system of a billion-dollar plane. Everything around the pilot can compute and react faster than a human can, so the human becomes the soft point or slow processing point of the supersonic weapons system. Computers will now be faster than even the most impatient users could possibly demand. Supermen and superwomen, all faster than a speeding bullet at the keyboards, trying to go faster than their computers—and failing in the effort.

All of this falls into the category of optical computer communications. It will allow significantly greater amounts of data to stream through networks to and from homes and offices at much faster speeds and at far less cost. This is an exponential equation of faster, cheaper, and more data all at once. This development also points to the possibility of a new generation of supercomputers that could share data internally at speeds much faster than today, which is staggering considering the speeds at which they currently operate.

We now live in the Shift Age, a time when the speed of change has accelerated so much that it has actually become part of the environment. A lot of people are unnerved by this ever-increasing speed that shows up in our lives, particularly in technology. Just go with the flow; there is no other choice. The trend lines for speed, power, and market penetration for computers and wireless devices are practically vertical. We are approaching a time in the near future when a singularity can occur in terms of time, distance, speed, connectivity, and consciousness: a new dawn for humanity. We are not just living in interesting times, as the Chinese proverb supposedly says; we are living in transformative times.

• • •

Sometimes It Is Easy to See the Future: Is It Real?

November 14, 2006

In many areas it might be difficult to predict the future, but in the area of technology the future can be readily seen. The speed of technological invention moves so quickly that we barely assimilate one breakthrough before another shows up to knock us back on our heels. While these innovations provide a glimpse of our future, they can be disorienting because they show us that the present we are struggling to accept will soon be outdated.

Last week NVIDIA Corporation made a major product announcement that has profound implications for supercomputing, gaming, and virtual reality. NVIDIA introduced its next-generation processor that has a capability of three trillion mathematical operations per second. To put that in historical perspective, the first mainframe computer, the ENIAC, built in 1946, performed 50,000 calculations per second. Ten years later the IBM 704 mainframe performed 400,000 per second. By 1982 the number had grown to 100 million for the most powerful mainframe computers in the world. So this new processor just by itself is 30,000 times faster than the most powerful mainframe of 25 years ago. In addition, this new processor will have 681 million transistors, more than twice as many as the current fast processors on the market. That probably means that each processor has more transistors than all the transistor radios produced worldwide in the 1950s.

This new processor, the GeForce 8800, is a graphics processing unit (GPU) and will be priced at $599. This and prior GPUs primarily serve the video gaming industry. Entertainment and media have recently and increasingly turned to the gaming industry for models. With NVIDIA's announcement, it is clear that gaming computer developments are impacting the general world of computing, which in recent years was beginning to think Moore's Law might come to an end. This convergence of graphics processors and conventional microprocessors looks to once again accelerate processing speeds in computers for years to come. In fact, this new development points to smaller computers having the computing speed of the supercomputers of the past decade. These have been the very fast computers that have been used for mega simulations and projections. At a store near you in just a few years.

The other key breakthrough coming, thanks to the GeForce 8800 processor, is that, finally, computer-generated imaging will approach photographic realism. The potential this will unleash is almost beyond comprehension. I remember a conversation I had several years ago with the most brilliant computer-generated imagery (CGI) artist I know. At the time he was creating and rendering photorealistic images of food products for major corporations. He told me that he could use CGI to create a photorealistic image of almost anything, with one big exception: a human face. He said that someday technology would solve that problem. When it did, who would need models or actors?

That day is soon to arrive. In fact, to highlight this very point, NVIDIA Corporation, at its unveiling of this new processor, showed an unnervingly real simulation of an actress. Just think of the implications for entertainment, fashion, and media companies. We can now move from the world of CGI newsrooms to CGI anchors and reporters. Stars could license full-motion replicas of themselves for any number of commercial and entertainment uses. The impact on pornography and sports simulation will be transformative.

In the next decade we will all be able to replicate ourselves into life-like avatars for any broadband enterprise we might be engaged in. Of course, the immediate beneficiary of this breakthrough will be the gaming industry, where speed and realism will soon take a giant leap ahead. High-end video games have come close to replicating known actors and presenting realistic characters already. Soon there will be games that seem as real as the movies they mimic. In the not-too-distant future, we will be able to insert lifelike images of ourselves in the video games we play.

To paraphrase the famous Memorex ad, "Is it real, or is it real?" So, in just a few years, when someone tells you to come back to reality, a valid response might be, "Which one?"

• • •

Cell Phones Are Transformative

December 8, 2006

It can be argued that the three most transformative technologies of the last 20 years are the personal computer, the Internet, and the cell phone, and I want to look at the third now.

As is often the case, a look into the future first entails a look back to the past. In 1984 there were 25,000 cell phones sold in the United States. In 1990 that number had grown to1,888,000 units sold; 52,600,000 units were sold in the year 2000—a million phones a week! And that number has continued to go up. Today, in a country of 300 million people—including infants, young children, and the aged—there are over 210 million active cell phone accounts. We all have cell phones. A number of people, like me, have two. So the cell phone is truly ubiquitous in the United States. This means cell phones are a commodity; in fact, a great number of people get them free with a service plan.

Twenty years ago, most of us had two phones, one at work, one at home, both connected to the wall. Our phone conversations were therefore placed-based, and, if we were out and about, there was always the pay phone. Remember those? Back then, no one ever called you up and said, "Where are you?" That's now one of the most frequently asked questions when the phone is answered. I don't need to talk about all the aspects of cell phones that have been written about ad nauseam, but I do want to stress that we now operate with a level of connectedness that has never existed before in history. This connectedness changes behavior, speeds up communications, and contributes to the accelerated speed of change in our society.

The explosive growth of cell phones in the United States that the above numbers describe has been equaled if not exceeded in every developed country of the world. What is really interesting is that this growth model is now occurring in developing and third-world countries. The current growth curves in Africa and Asia are very similar to those of the 1990s in developed countries. There are now 6 million new subscribers a month in India, and 5.25 million new subscribers a month in China. When these growth rates get projected out to 2010 and 2015, it is almost certain that the vast majority of nations in the world, including sub-Saharan countries, will have a majority of their citizens using cell phones. This is nothing less than transformative. Some of the countries that will have greater than 50-percent penetration of cell phones to people are the same ones that a couple of decades ago had less than 10 to 20 regular phones per 100 people. Think about how much our lives in the

United States have changed with cell phones. Now imagine it from a base where only one in five people had landline phones, and you can begin to see transformation at work—and play.

When more than 50 percent of the people in the world can call each other no matter where they are, a shift begins to occur. Compare today's reality of being able to reach potentially a billion people on their cell phones in a matter of seconds with the reality of 175 years ago, when the fastest means of communication was the speed of the Pony Express. That was horse speed, point to point. Now we have a billion plus points immediately connectable to each other. This is why I believe that we are approaching a coming shift in our evolutionary journey in the next 20 to 30 years.

Several ancient societies, including the Mayan civilization notably, had prophesies that the world as we know it would end in the year 2012. These prophesies were not about death, destruction, and catastrophes of biblical proportion. They predicted the world *as we know it* would end. When these prophesies were made centuries ago, human communication was completely contained by time and distance. The aha moment for me came when I realized that the trend lines for cell phones, computers, Internet use, and live satellite television show that the vast majority of humanity will have access to one if not several of these technological innovations in the years between 2010 and 2015, thereby essentially eliminating time and distance from human communication. Could it actually be 2012?

The world in 2012 will have changed from how the Mayans knew it. Time and distance will have ceased to exist in the realm of human communication. The Mayans could not have conceived of the cell phone, but they did predict what the cell phone was going to help usher into the world.

The cell phone, that gadget in your hand that is so indispensable to you, is one of the agents of change that is moving us toward an evolution shift in the decades ahead. Check back with me in the year 2013, so I can say, "I told you so!"

• • •

The Future of Video Games

December 12, 2006

In the last 10 years, video gaming has gone from a peripheral social phenomenon for teenage boys to a central feature in today's media and entertainment. Movies based on video games have been produced. TV executives talk about bringing the interactive gaming experience to television programming. Advertisers create games to position their brands. Advertising in video games is growing at a faster rate than in almost any other medium today. The sales revenue of the video game industry is greater than theatrical movies. Virtual reality, one of the biggest things in today's Internet world, can be traced to video games. Gaming is a major part of today's media and entertainment.

As all gamers and anyone consuming media today know, a console war is being waged. Last year Microsoft came out with the Xbox 360, the most powerful, integrated game console ever. With global online connectivity, it allows gamers around the world to play and compete together. It was embraced and deemed a huge success. A year later the other two major players in the console wars have introduced their products. Sony, the winner five years ago with its PlayStation 2, came out with its much anticipated and delayed PlayStation 3. The same week the number three player, Nintendo, came out with its radically different Wii. In a surprisingly short time, a winner has emerged, and it is the Wii.

The PlayStation 3 was a year late, made promises it did not deliver on, and is expensive. The executive who oversaw its development and launch has been relieved of his duties. The PlayStation continued down the path of evermore complex games with higher-quality graphics played with increasingly complex controllers. Most new games take a major time commitment to play because of their complexity. This approach focused on experienced gamers. The business plan was to compete with the Xbox 360 on all fronts.

Nintendo's strategy for the Wii is completely different. Nintendo decided that growth for video gaming lay in attracting non-gamers to join the fun. This meant developing a whole new system that doesn't rely on the now-high barrier of complex controllers. The Wii is radically different. The handheld controller is similar to a TV remote in its wand-like design. It can be moved through the air, and that motion is simulated on screen. Think about playing a video game of tennis. Instead of using your thumbs to execute a backhand, you wave the wand as though you were actually swinging your tennis racquet. Think about sword fighting and waving the controller through the air as if you were wielding a sword. It even sounds like more fun.

The controller is radically different, and so is the game design. Playing the games even for a short time is intended to be enjoyable. Ease of use and no major time commitment lower the barriers to non-gamers. Since there are more non-gamers than gamers, industry growth comes from transforming non-gamers into gamers. Early sales reports indicate that there are a lot of women and people over 30 buying the Wii consoles.

Another reason I think the Wii is the big winner is that, in addition to being attractive to non-gamers such as myself, experienced gamers are really excited about it. My 20-year-old son, who has been playing video games since the age of 8, told me he is more excited about the Wii than any other new gaming console he can remember. His friends who are gamers feel the same way and have all chosen to get the Wii, not the PlayStation 3. To them the Wii feels like an innovation that will lead to an entirely different experience than the existing one, which they are quite happy to continue playing. Because the Wii is wireless, whenever it's is plugged in, it can receive free updates.

It looks like Nintendo really does have a winner on its hands. Any new product that can attract experienced, sophisticated users and neophytes at the same time is a breakthrough.

Why is the Wii the future of video gaming? First, it opens up the market to new users. Second, in our ever-faster culture where time is a premium, it allows people to play for a short time and be satisfied. Third, it more closely correlates body movement and the game experience itself. It is this last point that I sense will be its greatest contribution. It feels like the Wii is the early beginnings of humans physically interacting with virtual worlds. Ten or twenty years from now, when we have immersive, interactive virtual worlds, the Wii may well be looked back on as the device that prepared us for this new, exciting plane of human experience.

There has been a great deal of interest in the new area of online virtual worlds such as Second Life. They are the beginning of the virtual world future that we will visit increasingly. However, they are only part of the equation, as they are all accessed by the computer, so the experience is driven by a keyboard and a mouse. This means they are conceptual and projective in nature. The Wii experience, while much more visually simplistic, is nevertheless the first widely available opportunity for humans to physically exert themselves on two different planes at the same time. In the *Matrix*-oriented, cyber worlds of the future, where travel, sports, and sex can all be a sensorial and physical experience, it will be the Wii that will looked on as the beginning of it all. The Wii will be to those future cyber worlds what Pong was to the video games that followed.

. . .

Technology Advances, Privacy Declines

December 15, 2006

One of the trade-offs we seem to have accepted during the past 20 years is a loss of privacy. None of us says we approve, but we have embraced technology in such a way that a diminished sense of privacy has occurred. The portability of storage and computing is a major reason. The easier storage devices and laptops are to carry, the higher probability of theft.

It was revealed the other day that a laptop with personnel records for 382,000 Boeing employees was stolen. This was the third time in 13 months that this has occurred with Boeing. Boeing is not the only company where this has happened. Laptops are portable and easy to put into a briefcase or bag. Someone goes up for another cup of coffee at Starbucks or leaves her desk to go to the bathroom, and in a few seconds the laptop and all the data on it are stolen. We enjoy the fact that we can have a computer with us wherever we are. The freedom to work wherever and whenever we want is a very empowering thing, something that didn't exist 20 years ago.

In the 1960s and 1970s, computing equaled mainframe computing. Companies and universities had these large machines that were in air-conditioned, controlled-access environments. Records were kept for all activities, and people dressed in white coats. It looked and felt like the religion of the mainframe. Yes, you could probably steal a computer tape, but you would need another mainframe computer to access the data. This is so different from today when every desk has a PC and laptops are everywhere.

The other key development is the Internet and the fact that these computers are connecting to it. This connectivity allows remote access from practically anywhere. Firewalls become challenges to hackers. Identities stolen from computers via the Internet can be almost instantaneously monetized. It seems like every day there is an article or story in the media about identity theft. So our highly connected lives open us up to risk.

And to tracking. What Web sites we visit on the Internet. What we buy. Who we communicate with and what we say. With massive use of wireless, we have grown accustomed to using public wireless hot spots for our most personal communications and transactions. We learned a decade ago that cell phones were less secure than landlines, yet that certainly didn't compel us to stop using them. In fact, cell phone usage has exploded.

Entirely new businesses such as consumer virus protection software providers and security gurus have emerged to help companies protect their data and confidential information. We want to be connected *and* protected. If you truly want to keep your communications private, think of the mafia movies you've seen. To avoid being bugged at home or at the office or being wiretapped, mafia dons would meet on a park bench or take a walk on a construction site to discuss "business." Once you move to mostly electronic communications, you increase the risk of intrusion, observation, or theft. Hey, what's so bad about sitting on a park bench on a sunny day?

• • •

Berkeley and Nanotechnology

January 25, 2007

Nanotechnology is one of the "next big things" in our future. People have elevated it to a level of near worship as the way to solve problems and revolutionize a number of areas of human life. Nanotechnology certainly has that potential, but it will take us into uncharted areas, and we must be cognizant of both benefits and potential liabilities.

Basically nanotechnology is an application of existing science and manufacturing at the atomic level. Nanoparticles are clusters of atoms and molecules, used in an ever-increasing range of invisible products and microscopic manufacturing methods and measured in nanometers, or billionths of a meter. Promoters of nanotechnology predict it might transform everything from energy production to health care, using microscopic particles to cure diseases in the body without surgery. Currently, however, it is being used in more mundane applications such as stain-resistant clothing.

Ever since I first learned of this new field, I've been concerned with the side effects or unintended consequences of this new technology. The environmental movement taught us about the interrelatedness of all things on our wonderful planet. We now look at things from a global and holistic perspective. It is this perspective that gives pause when thinking about nanotechnology. What might we inadvertently unleash while searching for miracle cures at the microscopic level?

DDT was first used during World War I, and later became the first widely used pesticide to protect agricultural crops. Post-war it was hailed as a miracle, as it greatly increased per-acre yield in many areas of farming. Our eyes were on the benefits and not on the unintended consequences. Rachel Carson made the unintended consequences clear in *The Silent Spring*,[1] one of the greatest environmental books of all time: DDT causes cancer in humans and has many deleterious effects on animals. As a result, DDT was ultimately banned. The key lesson learned was that chemical compounds put into the ecosystem cannot be controlled, contained, or managed. A success over here can create a disaster over there.

So this brings me to a wonderful article last week in the *New York Times* about Nabil Al-Hadithy.[2] Al-Hadithy is the hazardous waste manager of Berkeley, that unique city in California that since the Free Speech Movement in the 1960s has been on the front lines of social and cultural change and regulation. Nanotechnology became a concern for Al-Hadithy three years ago when a federal research lab in town filed an environmental impact statement for building "a molecular foundry" to make nanoparticles. He sent the lab a long list of questions that started with the question, "What the heck is a nanoparticle?" Since the answer was so complex, Al-Hadithy, fulfilling his responsibility to protect the citizens of Berkeley from the perils of hazardous waste, came up with his own answer and submitted a regulation to the city council.

Last month the city council adopted his regulation, making Berkeley the first governmental body in the United States, and most likely the world, to explicitly regulate enterprises that make or use nanoparticles. Berkeley citizens have long been skeptical about commercial enterprise's ability to anticipate disaster and have therefore encouraged their governmental agencies to stand tall in this regard. The new regulation requires businesses to identify all materials they produce or use with a dimension of 100 nanometers or less. In addition, they must fully disclose what they know about the possible toxicity of the particles and their procedures for monitoring, processing, and disposing of them.

I am very supportive of and excited about the potential of nanotechnology. My only concern is the real possibility of unintended consequences. So, with a big grin and a sense of gratitude, I tip my hat to Mr. Al-Hadithy and the city of Berkeley, California, for again focusing our attention on an important issue long before it becomes mainstream.

• • •

A Cell Phone Milestone

January 30, 2007

The cell phone, the personal computer, and the Internet are the three most transformative technologies of the last 20 years, as they have altered the fundamental concepts of time and space as it relates to human communication.

The interesting current phenomenon is that the growth rates of cell phone usage in developing countries are now rivaling the growth rates experienced in developed countries during the 1990s. There are 6 million new subscribers a month in India, and 5.25 million a month in China. In these two countries that does not just mean people moving from landlines to cell phones. It also means people having phones for the first time.

One billion cell phones were sold in 2006, the first time that has ever happened. Nokia led the pack with 300 million sold and achieved the milestone of 100 million sold in the last quarter of the year. Given that there are 6 billion people in the world and a large number of them are either children under 10 or live in extreme poverty, these numbers are amazing. One of the reasons is that cell phones have become a commodity.

When Motorola began selling the DynaTAC—the world's first commercial handheld cell phone, often referred to as "the brick"—it cost $4,000, which was about 10 percent of the average annual family income at that time. Now Motorola sells its iconic Razr phone for less than $100, and, if you don't really care about style, you can get a free phone with a two-year service agreement. In the developing world, the majority of phones are sold for less than $50.

This brings up an interesting point about transformative technologies. When first introduced and through the first few product cycles, they transform society because of their inherent qualities. Cell phones allow us to make calls regardless of where we are; we are no longer tied to some cord attached to a wall. Computers transform how we work and how productive we can be. The Internet is the greatest agent of disintermediation in the history of humanity. That is the first wave of transformation.

The second wave of transformation occurs when the price drops so low that market penetration dramatically rises. Then the inherent qualities of these technologies are amplified by an exponential increase in people using them. A million people using cell phones in the United States does not transform communications except for those million people. But 220 million cell phone accounts transform communications in the country. The same holds true for computers. The average price of a computer now is a fraction of what it was 20, or even 10, years ago. Now everybody has one. Finally, now that the cost of high-speed Internet connections has dropped, the percentage of households that have broadband access has crossed 50 percent. It is not a coincidence that the YouTube phenomenon happened at this time.

We are fast approaching the time when the majority of people living on earth will have cell phones. In what has been referred to as the Golden Triangle—North America, Western Europe, Japan, and Korea—76 percent of all people have cell phones. Outside this area, the penetration for the rest of the world is 27 percent, and that is where the growth will be the greatest. We are so used to our cell phones that we lose sight of what is actually going on: in just a few years, more than 50 percent of all humans on earth will be able to call each other regardless of where they are. That is a connectedness unimagined decades ago.

This connectedness is part of the vision I see unfolding during the next 20 to 30 years. It is part of the coming evolution shift that might well transform humanity. We might well be approaching one of the most historically seismic periods in our relatively short time on this planet. And that communications device of convenience you hold in your hand, the cell phone, will be a part of this coming change.

• • •

Moore's Law Lives On

February 2, 2007

Moore's Law is named for Gordon Moore, a co-founder of Intel. In the mid 1960s he predicted that transistor computing power would double every 24 months. (Moore initially posited 24 months and then shortened the cycle to 18.) Ultimately, the popular translation of this hypothesis and subsequent predictions he made was that, in the development of computers, the power of the computer would double every 18 months and the price would decrease by half. This became a truism in the PC business and for three decades proved to be true.

In recent years people suggested that perhaps Moore's Law had run its course. Such exponential growth could not go on forever. It started to settle in as fact that we were coming to the end of this remarkable development cycle. We all had computers that were infinitely faster and more powerful than the ones we first used 20 or 30 years ago, and we were paying a fraction of the cost of these early machines. So, if Moore's Law had run its course, that was OK as the low-cost speed and power at our finger tips was just fine, thank you very much.

But I believe Moore's Law is not yet dead, and burial was premature. This week gave strong evidence that the law continues. Intel announced a breakthrough that allows chips to leak less current, paving the way for a new generation of faster and much more energy-efficient processors. IBM, in a case of dueling company press releases, also said that they, in partnership with Advanced Micro Devices, made the same breakthrough.

With the increasing miniaturization of the transistor switches on chips, current leaked due to thinner insulation. Chips have been made with silicon insulators (yup, that's where the name "Silicon Valley" comes from), which allowed energy leakage. Increasing the thickness of this silicon insulation lessened the leakage but lowered the electric charge, limiting performance. This was the problem facing the researchers at Intel. The solution was to replace the silicon insulation with a metal insulation called hafnium that not only prevents leakage but helps with current conductivity.

This may sound simple, but, at the miniature size of chip manufacturing, the laws of physics come into play in new, uncharted ways. The chip industry is currently manufacturing chips in 90-nanometer technology. This means that approximately 1,000 chips would fit in the width of a human hair. A year ago Intel reduced the scale to 65 nanometers, which was followed months later by the rest of the industry; these smaller chips will come to market soon. Intel is moving to a minimum feature size of 45 nanometers. This now brings the industry into an area called molecular computing technologies, where early research indicates that this scale could be reduced even further in the next few years.

It is predicted that these new chips will not only find their way into the computers we use but also into consumer electronic devices such as cell phones, PDAs, and music players, greatly increasing their power and ability to function at much higher levels and at faster rates. Just when we thought the revolution in speed, power, and miniaturization was slowing down, we can look ahead to it continuing into the foreseeable future. It really does border on the remarkable and unimaginable. It is further evidence that the speed of change is not slowing but continuing to accelerate.

The Information Age has been defined by technology. Gordon Moore, one of the founding fathers of our current computing technology, set forth a visionary prediction 40 years ago that became the map and metrics for the entire computing business and continues to this day breaking down the physics of manufacturing. We are all the beneficiaries of this phenomenon and will be for years to come. Moore's Law lives!

• • •

The iPhone Starts It Up Again

July 2, 2007

People started using computers outside the corporate research lab in the 1950s. The early computers created in garages were brought to market in the mid 1970s. The IBM PC came out in 1981. The 1990s saw the early explosive growth of the laptop, and the current decade is when the

PDA and other wireless devices took off. This 50-year history is punctuated by various breakthroughs in the computer/human interface. Each of these breakthroughs changed usage, behavior, and ultimately society.

Mainframe computing of the 1950s looked like a technological religion. Well-lit, air-conditioned rooms housed large computers run by systems analysts and trained computer operators. Access was highly restricted. Entering a room with one of these mainframes felt like entering the church of the computer. The output was printed on reams of computer paper (remember?) that was largely illegible to the average person. Interpretation was provided by professionals.

When the Apple and later the IBM PC came out, humans could interact directly with small computers that sat on desktops with keyboards and screens. The screens were largely monochromatic and filled with alphanumeric language that needed some training to be intelligible. Later the mouse was added, which allowed windows, screens, and scrolling. Color and high-resolution screens soon followed. It was no longer necessary to have training to run a computer. This increasing ease of use—as much as small size, portability, and lowered cost—drove the incredible explosion in computer sales. When using a computer became easy and fun, sales took off. Computer use moved from the technological acolytes to the population as a whole. Just think how many fewer people would be using computers if there were no mouse attached.

The new iPhone is a seminal product; it brings an entirely new experience of easy and fun interface to millions of people. While the verdict on all aspects of the product is still out, it is clear that the touch screen is the most fascinating feature. It is how the product sells. Other phone manufacturers will be forced to keep pace and create touch screens and other cool human/device interfaces. Because of the high-profile hysteria surrounding the release of the iPhone, in addition to any of its unique features, it will serve as a significant marker in the ongoing history of human/computer interface.

One of the newer developments is something called surface, or multi-touch, computing. Heretofore only seen in science fiction movies like *Minority Report*, surface computing has the feel of a cool and revolutionary breakthrough. This technology will come to market in the next 12 months. In five years it will be used by millions. We can live in homes with touch-screen wallpaper in our lifetime: an environment of interactive surfaces everywhere we go. This will be transformational in many ways. Welcome to the fast-arriving future.

The beauty of the iPhone is that it will forever change our perception of what is possible in terms of human/machine interface. Who needs levers, buttons, or a computer operator when there is an intuitive interactive screen waiting to respond to any direction or touch? Imagine talking with a grandchild in 2020 and trying to explain to her that we actually used something called a computer keyboard.

• • •

A New Cell Phone Milestone

August 28, 2007

Currently there are more than 2.1 billion cell phone accounts in the world and more than 220 million in the United States. More people have cell phones than have computers or use the Internet. Globally there are some 15 to 20 million new cell phone accounts opened every month.

The cell phone has changed the way we communicate. We are available all the time, no matter where we are. Text messaging is a new form of communication that did not exist before the cell phone. We have experienced altered communication and behavior patterns as a result of this great technology. What is now clear is that the cell phone is dramatically changing how we view and use the landline phone.

Mediamark Research just released a study that reported that 14 percent of U.S. adults now live in households with one or more cell phones but no landline phone. That is an impressive statistic. What makes it a milestone is that it was also reported that 12.3 percent of adults live in a household with a landline phone, but no cell phone. For the first time in the United States, there are now more cell-phone-only households than landline-only households. The cell phone has moved from being something that was used outside the house to being the only phone. Conversely, landline phones can only be used in homes and in offices; they cannot encroach on the marketplace of portable cell phones.

This milestone is caused by two dynamics: the rapid growth of cell phones over the past fifteen years and the slow decline of landline phones in the last five years. These two trends will continue. A disproportionate number of the landline-only households are older-demographic households. I don't know any senior households that are cell-phone-only, but I do know a lot of twenty- or even thirtysomething households that are.

In addition to households, businesses are moving to the cell phone being the primary number. Most of us still have landlines for our business, but they are increasingly being listed second on business cards and rarely left on voicemail messages. They are beginning to feel almost as outdated as fax numbers in this age of e-mail and electronic attachments.

The larger context is the move toward wireless for all communications and electronic devices. Cell phones, PDAs, laptops, and wireless networks make us less limited by wires and cords for communication and increasingly entertainment. Please take a step back and reflect on the fact that the wireless state of affairs we now take for granted only existed in science fiction and in the vision of futurists just 30 years ago. The always available, always connected, always portable, ever-smaller, and evermore powerful wireless world that is our present was only in the future a couple of decades ago. See, how easily we can adapt to the future when it suits us?

CHAPTER 6:
ENERGY AND GLOBAL WARMING

SOCIETY IS ADDICTED to energy produced by fossil fuels. This addiction contributes to global warming, pollutes our precious environment, makes the United States dependent on foreign countries for its economic lifeblood, and appears untenable with the rising costs of fossil fuels.

We face a challenge and an opportunity. We must respond immediately to the urgent environmental issues. But, if we collectively accept the challenge, we have the chance to not only secure our continued survival on this planet but to also benefit from the innovative and economic by-products of our intervention.

The columns in this chapter provide an awareness of energy issues and environmental concerns, encourage commitment to solving the problems, and examine emerging solutions. Read as a whole, the chapter is an incitement to action before we reach the point of no return.

Incidentally, columns on this subject produced the most response from Evolution Shift blog readers. People are concerned about these issues and are angry about the federal government's lack of leadership.

Solving the Energy Problem and Saving Ourselves

May 3, 2006

The systemic societal addiction to petroleum is at the top of the list of important issues we now face. It, more than any other issue, affects the future of humanity. I believe we are approaching a choice that could determine how our history will be written 300 years from now. In the decades ahead, humanity might well have the opportunity to take the next major step in its evolutionary journey. If that occurs, it will be in part because we successfully handle the impending global energy crisis. Let's take a look at where we are and what might happen.

Most Americans, even if they are not baseball fans, understand what "three strikes, and you're out" means. You get three chances. Three chances to hit the ball, get on base, score a run, solve a problem, create an opportunity. Well, we are facing our third strike today.

The first strike was the OPEC oil embargo of 1973 and 1974, when in the short span of three months the price of oil and gasoline increased fourfold. Oil went from $3 to almost $12 a barrel, and gasoline went from $.30 to $1.20. What was the response? The Alaskan pipeline was approved, Americans frantically clamored for and then purchased smaller cars, and the economies of Europe and the United States went into a deep and gut-wrenching recession. We invented the word *stagflation* to describe our stagnant economies that suffered rampant inflation (remember 20-percent mortgage rates in 1979?). But no long-term solutions to the increasing dependency on oil, and on foreign oil, were put into place. We were all too entrenched in the status quo to shift. It was only a pocketbook issue, except for extreme environmentalists.

Strike two was 1981 when gasoline, measured in real dollars, peaked at more than $3 a gallon. This was another slam to the pocketbook of consumers and a drag on an economy in recession. Once again there were a lot of reactive policy conversations and economic hand-wringing. It took another almost 25 years until the price of gasoline at the pump again reached this price, adjusted for inflation. When the price receded, so did our discussion of long-term energy solutions.

It is interesting to look at historical government data on gasoline use and passenger cars. In 1950, on an annual basis, the average car in the United States was driven 9,060 miles, consumed 603 gallons of gas, and averaged 15 mpg. In 1972, the full year prior to the oil embargo, the numbers were 10,171 miles, 754 gallons, and 13.5 mpg (remember muscle cars?). In 1975, the first full year after the embargo, usage was down, at 9,309 miles, 665 gallons, and 14 mpg. In 1982, when the price of gasoline subsided from its all-time high, the numbers were 9,050, 535, and 16.9: usage down, consumption down, mpg up.

Every single year since then, mileage has gone up, gas consumption per car has stayed about the same, and mpg has gone up. In 2003 compared to 1982 mileage was up 35 percent to 12,242 miles, gas per car was up 3 percent at 550 gallons, and mpg was up 32 percent to 22.3.

The real problem is that the number of cars in the United States quadrupled from 1950 to 2000. This was not just due to population growth as measured by number of households but also to the number of cars per household. In 1960 the percentage of households that had three or more cars was 2.5 percent; in 2000 it was 18.3 percent. Since strike one and strike two, we have dramatically increased the number of cars and the amount of miles driven per car. This has not been offset by a commensurate increase in mpg. It is interesting to note that the mpg figures have barely moved in the last 15 years. The conclusion is obvious: as individuals we are driving a lot more, and as a nation we lost our resolve to dramatically increase mpg.

Strike three is right now. In the United States gas is up over the 1981 price of $3 per gallon and climbing, mpg has flattened out, there is much more demand for petroleum around the world, supplies are at risk due to political and terrorist situations, and our government has only come up with election-year grandstanding. The president and vice president are both former oil men and so far have only promised to seek out price gougers, the Democrats want to rescind the 18.4 cents tax per gallon, and the Republicans want to give us each a $100 check before the fall elections. Leadership? Show me!

So, how do we prevent a strikeout? Three areas: actions to take in the present, strategies to initiate for the future, and a necessary change in values and thinking.

In the present, we need an all-of-the-above attitude. Conservation through a conscious change in behavior, primarily use of automobiles, public transport, carpooling, walking, and biking? Yes. A change in how we buy cars, buying only those with highest mpg ratings? Yes. Support for and growing use of ethanol, other mixed fuels, and electric cars. Yes? Legislation to drive a dramatic increase in mpg figures for all vehicles? Yes. Accept as fact that we are at the global petroleum production peak right now and that, in the coming decade, demand will increasingly outstrip supply? Yes. An absolute voter intolerance for any elected official who does not support the long-term goal of decreasing use of petroleum and finding viable alternative energy sources? Yes.

To protect our future, we need mobilization and resolve. Mobilize the United States through a government-supported, entrepreneur-led "space program" (in the old 1960s meaning of the term) to decrease our use of petroleum by 50 percent in the next 10 years. This includes tax benefits for investments in alternative energy and technology that increases efficient use of petroleum, tax benefits for automotive manufacturers that deliver the highest mpg per vehicle class, tax deductions for people who can document lower petroleum energy usage on a year-to-year basis, and a massive information program on petroleum usage and conservation.

Create a completely open and unrestricted marketplace for energy innovation. Allow and replicate Silicon Valley's technology history of the past 30 years in the field of energy. No restrictions that serve current vested interests in the status quo.

We also need to change our thinking and values regarding energy. Americans need to change how they think about and how they value the concepts of space and distance. Space is increasingly expensive to heat or cool, and distance is increasingly expensive to travel. The size of the average new house in the United States has grown dramatically in the last three decades while energy costs have skyrocketed. Is this smart? No. Is this self-indulgent? Yes. Suburbia has given way to exurbia. Is this intelligent planning? No. How far one is willing to travel in a daily commute should become a more important part of the analysis of whether to take a job. We must begin to think of space and distance as global citizens, as United States citizens, not as indulgent individuals.

We need to look to the Internet and wireless technologies for how they can help us deal with this worsening energy crisis: frictionless, gasless commerce that every day becomes less place-based and more content- and transaction-driven. Do we need more shopping malls or more bandwidth? More highways or more communications backbone?

I am optimistic about the long-term outcome here. It is ultimately a matter of survival for all of us on earth. The economic riches that will come to those who create alternative, yet-to-be imagined energy sources are unlimited; they dwarf any other financial opportunity today. Survival and economic gain are two of the strongest drivers of human behavior.

There are going to be some rough, uncomfortable, and expensive lessons ahead for us, until we re-chart our course. The questions are: how long will it take us to truly realize our survival is at stake, and how much pain and social disruption must we endure until we come to that realization?

• • •

Europe All the Time, New York When It Needs To

August 17, 2006

On a recent trip to Europe I was reminded that Europeans are more conservation-oriented and energy-efficient than Americans. The lights in hotel hallways are off until you walk by a sensor or push a button; they go on for two minutes and then go off again. Motion sensors everywhere turn lights on in hallways, stairwells, and public spaces. In Munich I saw something for the first time: public escalators that don't move until someone walks onto them and passes a motion detector. All over downtown Munich there were non-moving escalators, waiting.

Then there are the small cars, the tiny two-seater sedans that even if not electric must get close to 50 miles per gallon. Then, of course, all the bicycles. In Berlin and much more so in Munich bikes seemed like the preferred mode of transportation. At a couple of suburban train stations, I saw literally hundreds of bicycles left by train commuters. (Guess there is also a difference in the level of theft between the United States and Europe!) Everywhere there were bicycles.

All of this made a real impression on me. It made me again realize how energy-indulgent we Americans are. Lights always on, escalators always moving whether they are being used or not, frigid air conditioning that drives people to wear sweaters inside during the summer, and everything big, big, big.

The week after I came back from Europe I took a trip to New York City during a record heat wave. For three days the highs were 95 to 102 degrees. This was two weeks after another heat wave when overuse of the electric grid had caused a blackout in some areas. To avoid another blackout, Mayor Bloomberg launched a major communications effort to ask people to turn off lights, to lower the output of air conditioners, and to do what they could to lessen electric use.

Guess what? Everybody seemed to respond, "Can do." New Yorkers rose to the occasion. I remember one day going in three different, large office buildings, and half of the lobby lights were off in every one. That same day I noticed that some of the track lighting in two different restaurants had been turned off. I was in several different office suites, and all of them had a noticeable number of ceiling lights switched off. So, when called on, Americans can act energy-intelligent. Granted the actions were to avoid something bad, another blackout, but people did seem to get a sense of purpose in these actions, a "we're doing our part" feeling.

Having just returned from Europe I couldn't but help see New York's problem through that filter. Hey, maybe the most energy-indulgent country in history can change and act with the intelligence of the Europeans. Treat energy as a valuable rather than disposable resource.

It is a valuable resource. We have only decades of petroleum left. We need to stretch that timeline as much as we can to buy time to make the discoveries and create the innovative inventions that can move us beyond a need for petroleum and to renewable sources of energy. Humanity can have an incredibly bright future—but only if this problem is solved.

There were two ingredients in the New York experience that perhaps Americans need to break their energy habits: fear and hands-on, well-communicated leadership. The fear of another blackout and Mayor Bloomberg's omnipresent messaging won the day in New York. Americans need to visualize what life would be like with $7 gas and regular blackouts. Truly see that vision, and use it as motivation to act differently.

As for the concerned, hands-on, visionary leadership, we all look to Washington to hopefully find some. Mobilize the country to win this effort similar to the home-front mobilization during World War II. Provide a vision, and therefore create the innovation, similar to the man-on-the-moon effort. To paraphrase a 1960s song about alienation: where have you gone John F. Kennedy, our nation casts it leaderless eyes to you?

• • •

A Walk on the Beach

August 28, 2006

As a futurist I spend a lot of time looking for patterns and forces that may develop into trends. This is just the way I look at the world, trying to connect the dots into patterns and directions that suggest the future. However, in some cases it doesn't take a futurist to spot a linkage between certain developments. Let me take you back a few days to a walk on the beach.

I was in Sarasota, Florida, to take care of my condo and to do a lot of writing and reading. As I always like to do when doing intensive writing and reading, I took a break to go for a long walk on the beach. Getting out of the car at the beach, I was hit with a powerful smell of dead fish and, within a couple of minutes, was suffering from shallow coughing: the telltale signs of a red tide. For those of you who don't know the term, a "red tide' is when there is a sudden bloom of algae in the ocean. The amount of algae explodes in quantity, sucking up all the oxygen from the water. The two immediate results are the death, due to lack of oxygen, of other flora and fauna in the water and the production of a mildly noxious gas that irritates the human respiratory system. The consequence is a beach littered with endless dead fish and mounds of seaweed and very few people. The lifeguards were wearing some sort of gas mask apparatus.

Now red tides regularly occur. As the local paper reported, however, this red tide came on the heels of a much larger one last year that covered 2,000 square miles and killed off most of the fish in Sarasota Bay. This increasing frequency provokes alarm. While state officials, probably with an eye on tourism, say they don't have enough information to determine an upward trend in red tides, scientists, looking at the same data the state is looking at, concluded these red tide blooms are 10 to 15 time worse than 50 years ago.

While on the beach I recalled a *New York Times* article I had read on the plane concerning a troubling dead zone off the coast of Oregon.[1] This is the fifth straight year that a dead zone has appeared off this coast, but this year it is the biggest, covering 1,200 square miles. The oxygen levels have been startlingly low. No fish can live in this zone. Dead zones occur in various places around the world, but five straight years off the Oregon coast is something new. Scientists say this has been predicted in models run to forecast the effects of global warming.

This line of thinking made me remember a news story about the number of brush and forest fires in the United States; the occurrence of these fires in recent years seems to be increasing. Thinking of heat made me think of the two weeks I spent in Germany this summer when temperatures hit record highs. On returning to the United States, I got to experience the record heat waves that were occurring across the country in early August.

It doesn't take much to connect these dots. Global warming immediately comes to mind—thanks for recent amplification to Al Gore and *An Inconvenient Truth*. But "global warming" is just a catchphrase for the larger issue of humanity's mindless trashing of the planet through overpopulation, rampant development, and a crackhead-like addiction to petroleum. It's not just about fuel-efficient cars, as almost every aspect of our economic society is based on cheap petroleum that is no longer cheap.

It is very clear to me that we are approaching two tipping points. One is the tipping point that I believe could occur in the next few decades when, if we don't act with urgency to save the planet for continued human occupancy, we will no longer be able to do so as the aggregated damage caused hits a point of no return. The second tipping point is that of awareness, desire, and commitment to save ourselves and what remains of biodiversity on this planet. I just hope the second point tips before we reach the point of no return.

If we want to continue to have nice days at the beach, we have to get to work—and soon.

. . .

Once Again It Starts in California

September 25, 2006

In the last half of the 20th century many of the major social, political, and cultural trends in the United States started in California. The worship of the car, the glorification of suburbia via sitcoms, surfing, music, the drug culture and counterculture, free speech and student protest, progressive public higher education, the Silicon Valley explosion of technological innovation, and, of course, right turn on red. Later the negative issues of traffic gridlock, illegal immigration, brownouts, and state budget deficits started first in California. Now, on one of the most fundamentally important issues of the day, the state has once again asserted its leadership position.

A couple of weeks ago the state legislators passed one of the most important pieces of legislation in recent memory: the California Global Warming Solutions Act of 2006. This is the first time any state has approved legislation that caps emissions for all economic sectors of the state. This legislation mandates that major industrial producers must reduce admissions by 25 percent by 2020. That means a reduction in annual carbon dioxide emissions by some 175 million tons. The inverse math is staggering: 700 million tons of carbon dioxide emissions every year in the state of California alone!

In a country where the federal (lack of) leadership is not only asleep at the wheel but has its foot on the gas pedal, it is wonderful to see a Republican governor and a Democratic legislature come together to start the absolutely essential process of changing our society's relationship to the planet. Simple, gas-drunk politicians have for too long equated pollution with economic growth, jobs, and an increasing tax base. It was determined in the preparation of this legislation that the global warming reduction effort would increase income by billions and would create tens of thousands of jobs. Developing green technologies, using innovation to lessen reliance on fossil fuels, and finding new ways of production will all lead to economic growth. One great aspect of this legislation is that any company that is a supplier to the State of California, whether in the state or not, must abide by these new regulations. That means this will have ramifications beyond the state line.

As my readers know, I firmly believe that the development of alternative fuel and renewable energy is the single largest economic opportunity in the history of humanity. Those who create alternatives to our current consumption of energy could realize incalculable wealth. When oil was first pumped from the ground in the latter part of the 19th century, the immediate market potential was tens of thousands of customers. The market potential for alternative fuels today is billions of customers.

But the State of California did not stop with this groundbreaking legislation. Last week, the State sued six automakers over vehicle emissions. Stating that global warming is causing California significant harm, the attorney general sued General Motors, Toyota, Ford, Honda, Chrysler, and Nissan, saying they created a public nuisance by collectively discharging 289 million tons of carbon dioxide into the atmosphere annually. It was stated in the lawsuit that these six companies were responsible for a fifth of the carbon dioxide emissions in the United States and a third of the emissions in California because of the great number of vehicles in the state.

Whether California wins this lawsuit or not, just the fact of it is significant. In the early days of the lawsuits against the tobacco companies, the prevailing thinking was that there was no chance that the tobacco companies would lose. The vast majority of auto executives have shown a woeful lack of leadership and global citizenship in the area of increased mpg, lowered emissions, and the development of hybrid and electric cars. Maybe the threat of a few lawsuits that could effectively bankrupt their companies might give them impetus to start to do what is clearly essential and what they should have been doing for the past 10 years.

I predict that 10 years from now the legislation that California passed this month and the lawsuit just filed will be seen as milestones. Let's hear it for the great State of California!

. . .

National Defense Becomes Green

October 31, 2006

The dramatic increase in gasoline prices over the summer combined with the perception that oil revenues fund terrorism created a new awareness of the need for the United States to import oil. It is now clear to a growing number of Americans that dependency on foreign oil compromises our security.

In a recent poll conducted by the Democracy Corps, a Democratic group, likely voters were asked what they thought were the two most important national security priorities for the government over the next few years.[2] Coming in first with 42 percent was reducing dependence on foreign oil. A distant second at 26 percent was combating terrorism. Third was the war in Iraq at 25 percent. Strengthening America's military came in at 12 percent. This means that the connection between oil and terrorism and the perception that America could at any time be brought to its knees by foreign oil-producing states has become the greatest security fear of voters.

Politicians pay attention to voters. Once again, the people are leading the politicians when it comes to a commonsense view of oil and the world. It has been clear since 9/11—when the Bush Administration told us that going shopping, instead of participating in a patriotic conservation effort, was the correct reaction to the attack—that this group of non-leaders has no stomach for an obvious, rational energy policy. Now that the voters say that energy independence is the number one security issue, even President Bush, along with a slew of other politicians, is scrambling to catch up to the electorate.

Since American politicians are so quick to campaign on a strong defense, the electorate is forcing them to become green if they want to get or stay elected. The vested interests of big oil and its influence on legislators are trumped by the vested interest of staying in office. This will ultimately lead to more governmental support of alternative energy and conservation and perhaps even some leadership on those topics. It is interesting that the electorate, as it did in the Dubai Ports incident, has taken over the political conversation and forced policy change.

It will be amusing to see how self-styled hard-liners on defense will embrace green policies now that they are clearly the most important long-term security issue. Self-reliance, that American virtue so eloquently written about by Emerson in the 1840s, is now the central building block of security policy. While the electorate sees this, the key question is what the individuals who make up this body politic will actually do in their lives to lessen dependency on oil. We have moved to a tipping point in the United States where energy has moved from a cost category in our minds to an issue of survival, survival of the country, and, long term, survival of humanity.

Americans may not yet be saying they will give up their energy-based lifestyle, but they are saying that they would like it run on something other than oil purchased from foreign countries. Imagine how different the world is going to look when petroleum is one of many sources of energy that we use every day. Imagine the possibility of renewable energy and an America that produces all that it needs. Being self-reliant and not funding terrorism. A transformative vision that is attainable with commitment, innovation, a bit of fear, and leadership.

• • •

Make Global Warming an Economic Issue

November 7, 2006

Last week the British government released the Stern report on global warming.[3] As those of you who read about it know, the report suggests that, without immediate and aggressive spending, global warming will reduce worldwide productivity on the scale of the Great Depression. The report, commissioned by the British government, is the most comprehensive study to date of the economic impact of global warming. The quick summary is that failure to act could cost up to 20 percent of lost income worldwide on an annual basis. Aggressive and immediate action to solve the problem would cost 1 percent of gross global domestic product.

Global warming has now been framed economically. Do nothing, and have economic consequences on the order of the Great Depression, consequences that would almost by definition lead to an open-ended depression, or take immediate action across the board at an estimated 1 percent additional cost. Not exactly a difficult decision to make, at least if you're looking at the situation with clarity. Of course, there are still people, and prominent U.S. politicians, who say that it's too expensive to cut greenhouse gases. We shouldn't let these ostrich-like approaches to this huge issue hold us back any longer. The scientists have weighed in on the fact that there is global warming, and now the economic consequences of the danger have been presented in a powerful way.

Economics is obviously a primary driver in the countries of the world. Economics seems to often trump other areas of life. Since this is the case, making global warming an economic issue for us all might be one way to develop the global will to solve this problem. The real possibility of suffering dire economic consequences has always been a good motivator. It is something that many people have felt, and those of us who had parents who grew up during the Great Depression have heard stories about how awful it was. This might be a more concrete way to get people to take action than the hard-to-imagine image of Manhattan and Florida under water.

The Stern report states that the current level of greenhouse gases is 54 percent higher than at the beginning of the Industrial Revolution (which was about 300 years ago, a tiny blip in humanity's time on the planet), and that figure could well double by 2035. Such an increase could raise average temperatures by close to four degrees Fahrenheit and a calamitous nine degrees Fahrenheit by the end of the century. According to the report, global warming would be most harshly felt by poor countries, but developed countries must be responsible for 60 to 80 percent of emissions reductions.

The report is optimistic in that it states, if we start to act immediately, we can turn global warming around. It cautions, however, that if humanity waits even a decade to begin, perhaps two decades at the outside, the consequences will be the dire ones suggested.

The only way to deal with the issue of global warming is through a comprehensive and coordinated international effort that so far has yet to take hold. Perhaps making the price of not taking this step a prolonged global depression might be the catalyst for more immediate action. We must all think about and speak about global warming as a coming economic catastrophe that can be prevented if we take action soon. We must all take action in our own lives to cut energy use, and we must bring this issue into the national and international discussion. Do nothing, and suffer the greatest depression in history. Politicians don't want to be responsible for that. To quote James Carville from the 1992 presidential campaign, "It's the economy, stupid!"

• • •

Three Cheers for Titanium Dioxide

December 1, 2006

This column goes into that age-old category of "learn something every day." As my readers know, I believe we must do everything we can to both find alternative sources of energy and slow down the accelerating global warming trend. One of the key ways to accomplish both of these is through technological innovation.

The other day I read an article in the *New York Times* that was nothing less than thrilling regarding technology and global warming.[4] Six years ago the architect Richard Meier designed a church in Rome. The dominant design element was curvilinear white concrete. To preserve the whiteness, the primary technical sponsor worked on a coating for the concrete. Six years later the coated concrete is as white as it was when constructed while other parts of the building have grayed due to atmospheric pollution. Now the thrilling part: the white pigment used actually "eats" surrounding smog!

It was determined through testing that construction materials that contain titanium dioxide, the key ingredient in the white pigment, destroy the pollutants found in car exhaust and heating emissions. In other words, titanium dioxide breaks down the nitrogen oxides that are emitted by burning fossil fuels. It is called photocatalytic cement. The maker of the pigment, Italcementi, has conducted numerous tests that have determined that some pollutants could be reduced by 20 to 70 percent. The reduction of pollutants is greatest within a distance of eight feet. In one test a 1,000-foot stretch of highway outside Milan, with a high level of vehicular traffic, was paved with titanium dioxide, and it was found that there was a 60-percent reduction of nitrogen oxides at street level.

This is not only a wonderful unintended consequence; it really is an innovative technological breakthrough of the highest order in our effort to cut down emissions that lead to global warming. Think about the concept of having the buildings and streets of cities treated with photocatalytic cement. Everyone walking down the street would be less than eight feet from sideways, streets, and buildings, so the pollution people inhale would be dramatically reduced. Through building codes, we could require that all concrete be coated with this material and that regular reapplications be mandatory.

The vast paving of the land in the United States and around the world contributes to global warming since all this asphalt and concrete retains heat and prevents water absorption. We can now take one of our more egregious assaults on the environment and negate it to some degree. Make all our building materials act like trees!

It will take dozens, if not hundreds, of such technological breakthroughs and their implementation to make substantial inroads in our effort to slow and ultimately reverse global warming. We must look at everything we do and consistently find ways to change our behavior and correct damage done. However, for each breakthrough we must celebrate a small victory. Three cheers for titanium dioxide!

· · ·

A Man Who Is Working to Save the Planet

April 10, 2007

Last week I wrote about an incredible energy conference hosted by the Foundation for the Future. As one of a select few invited to observe and participate in the conference, I had the incredible experience of listening to and meeting with 15 of the top thinkers and scientists in the world today on the subject of the future of energy. The brilliance of the participants and the level of discussion were so great that I decided it must be shared with my readers. This column will give you insight into our energy future, as seen through the eyes, mind, and research of one of the most well-known, accomplished energy experts alive today.

Russ George is a man who is doing what he can to save the planet, literally. In addition, he is an entrepreneur who hopes that by helping us to help him save the planet, his company can make money. (As my regular readers know, I fully support this, as there is a need to counterbalance the status quo of the energy business with new ways to make money that provide help to the planet and develop a future of sustainable and renewable energy.) Russ is founder and CEO of Planktos (http://www.planktos.com), a company that strives to restore ecosystems and slow climate change. Planktos is the leading ecorestoration firm in the world that generates carbon offsets in two ways: by restoring plankton populations in the world's oceans and by planting new "climate forest parks."

Plankton and trees absorb great amounts of carbon dioxide, CO_2, which is put in the atmosphere by humans, particularly through the use of petroleum-based energy. Plankton beds in the ocean and forests of trees on land consume and therefore offset the CO_2 waste products we put in the biosphere. Hence the term "carbon offset," whereby anyone can spend money to help cultivate plankton beds and tree forests, compensating for the CO_2 she generates.

Houle: Russ, how much CO_2 would one of my readers generate per year?

George: An average adult has a carbon footprint of about five tons per person per year in average homes. Travel footprints for a car are about six tons per year, though large SUVs are at least double that figure. A typical family of four in the United States has a carbon footprint of about 20 tons per year, which includes one car. [Note to readers: even the Toyota Prius generates 3.4 tons of carbon per year.]

Houle: So what can this family do to offset its CO_2 waste? How does Planktos help?

George: Planktos profitably employs green plants in our trees-and-seas projects to remove CO_2 and sells that work to people at $5 a ton. This means that a family of four with a gentle living style can totally erase its carbon footprint for $100 a year. If your readers want to become carbon-neutral, they can visit the Planktos Web Store at http://www.planktos.com/store. They will receive a wall certificate and a car sticker that can be put on the inside of a window showing the car is carbon-neutral for the year.

Houle: How do you create the growth of ocean plankton?

George: Stated simply, we put iron dust into the ocean. That needs an explanation. Iron is used by plants to greatly enhance photosynthesis. Plants on land or near land always have more than adequate supplies of iron. Plants in the distant ocean, the pelagic ocean, only get iron from dust that travels thousands of miles via the wind. Due to several changes in the biosphere, there is less iron being blown from the land to the ocean.

We grind up iron into extremely small particulates and then seed the oceans. This is a dirt-cheap solution we call eco-judo, turning bad into good. CO_2 in the air and ocean is bad unless you happen to be a growing green plant, in which case you see it as plant food. By seeding plankton blooms with iron, we provide the essential nutrient that will allow these blooms to grow, flourish, and consume ever-greater amounts of CO_2.

Houle: So you could be called "the Johnny Appleseed of plankton." Right?

George: If you say so.

Houle: What about the trees you plant?

George: The trees are in new forests in the national parks of the European Union. Our subsidiary KlimaFa ("Climate Tree" in Hungarian) is working with the Hungarian government to have trees planted by unemployed workers who are trained and earn a new living being ecoforest workers. We begin to plant 25,000 acres in a few weeks. We have an additional 200,000 acres lined up in Hungary and many times that amount in other countries in the EU. This is a "darling" project of the EU with support and interest of major international institutions and development banks. These forests will remove millions of tons of CO_2 from the air.

Houle: Russ, please tell the triage metaphor you used at the conference regarding global warming.

George: OK, imagine we are traveling down the highway, and we come across a poor victim lying on the road, someone who has sustained severe injuries. The first things we would do are to check breathing, stop the bleeding, get the patient stable, look for the cause of the injury, and then get medical help for the victim. Well, if we think of the victim as planet earth, that is what we should be doing, yet here we are arguing about whether the victim is injured or not, what or who was to blame, whether we should do anything or just wait and see what happens.

Houle: Please also tell the operating system metaphor for planet earth.

George: Well, first of all, since 72 percent of the surface of the planet is water, it should really be called "planet ocean." Anyway, think of the human race and its use of fossil fuel as a very misbehaving software application on our planetary ecosystem of life. That aberrant software application is firing so many errors back to the root operating system—the oceans in particular—that the operating system is beginning to malfunction. Like any good operating system, ours is robust and self-correcting, but, if you keep pounding in application errors, the application is likely to crash, upsetting the operating system. If the operating system cannot self-correct, it will have no choice but to reboot. In this case the operating system called planet ocean will reboot and reset itself back millions of years.

Houle: What is the possibility of that happening?

George: Well, the ocean acidification from CO_2 is so serious and way over the tipping point that, if we don't help to correct it, and fast, it is possible that by the latter part of this century, the most important ocean green plants will literally dissolve in the acid oceans. It is the simple first principal chemical reaction: $H_2O + CO_2 = H_2CO_3$, or carbonic acid. This is why it is so important to not only cut back on emissions but to grow vast new plankton blooms in the oceans and trees on land to combat the billions of tons of CO_2 we are putting into the atmosphere every year.

Houle: We have run out of space. Thank you!

George: Thank you. I urge your readers to go to the Web site and buy the appropriate amount of carbon offsets so they are living carbon neutral.

Houle: Now that is something everyone should do. I did.

• • •

We Have Only Just Begun

April 17, 2007

I have written several times that the United States crossed the tipping point on global warming in 2006. It has only been in the last year that the understanding of the global warming issue has become mainstream in this country. Two years ago it was environmentalists who spoke of it; now almost everyone does.

As someone who has long been concerned that this country and the rest of the world are marching blindly forward toward an overheated planetary nightmare, I am happy to see almost everywhere I look the subject of global warming. Last week the cover of *Time Magazine* was "The Global Warming Survival Guide." The current issue of *Vanity Fair* is the second annual "Green Issue." Last week Discovery Networks announced it's converting one of its networks into a "green" network. Starting today, Home Depot will introduce labeling for nearly 3,000 products that conserve energy or promote energy conservation, sustainable forestry, and clean water. Home Depot expects to increase the number of products to 6,000, or 12 percent of its products, by 2009. In addition, these products will get preferential treatment such as prominent shelf-positioning and being highlighted in marketing efforts. Good work *Time*, *Vanity Fair*, Discovery Networks, and Home Depot.

Now the truth of the matter is that everyone is learning it pays to be green. Media outlets, retail chains, and even car companies are falling over themselves to be green, to be environmentally friendly, to become carbon-neutral, to contribute percentages of sales to environmental organizations. Everybody wants to "out green" the competition in hopes of increasing readers, viewers, and customers. This is all good. It is a good thing to make global warming an economic issue. It really doesn't matter to me whether these initiatives are altruistic or financially motivated. New patterns are developing; more people every day are getting onboard; the momentum is accelerating so much that in a couple of years the competitive advantage will be diminished. The inverse will become true: if you are not clearly doing your part to help slow down global warming, you will be punished in the marketplace. An even worse fate will fall to those companies that are discovered to be playing the global warming PR game without committed follow-through.

This explosion of awareness and action is a wonderful thing, but we, as individuals, as Americans, as consumers, as companies, as voters, have only just begun. The goal is to slow down and then reverse humanity's contribution to global warming. The adverse affects of humans have not yet been measurably slowed. Even if tomorrow all our greenhouse emissions declined, there are still years of warming ahead because of what we have already done, because of what already has been lost. So we have only just begun.

It may feel good to talk about your conservation efforts at a party or to show the world you drive a hybrid, but don't get smug. Even a Toyota Prius produces more than three tons of carbon dioxide emissions (as opposed to the automotive average of six tons). The goal is not to feel good, though; if that is a nice by-product, fine. All of us can do more, all of the time.

Currently it costs more to be green. We pay more for a hybrid than a less green car in the same class. We pay more for fluorescent bulbs than incandescent bulbs. Installing solar panels takes 12 years to pay back. All of this will be temporary. We must now pay more, but the marketplace will change as prices fall and green becomes the new normal. This is a short-term price to pay for the planetary damage we've done through the years.

Do what you can to make sure the politicians you might vote for know your vote is conditional on how committed, knowledgeable, and leading-edge they are on the issues of global warming, energy independence, and sustainable energy. Some of us may press on such issues as gay marriage, abortion, or the war in Iraq; all of us need to press on these energy issues.

It is absolutely wonderful that we have gone through the tipping point. It is the first step. We have only just begun.

• • •

Change the Language, Change the Thinking

May 8, 2007

We are all more aware of global warming than we were years ago. As a country we passed through the tipping point of awareness in the last year. We have a better understanding of what it is we each do to contribute to global warming, and a number of us have taken action to lessen those contributions as much as possible. We now need to change some of the language we use, as it will help us to continue to change our thinking and our behavior.

I have heard relatively environmentally aware people speak about their cars' mpg rating. People talk about "doing their part" by driving a 30-mpg vehicle or buying a hybrid to help cut down on harmful emissions and to save on gasoline. That is great, no question. What is needed now is for those people and the rest of us to not rest on the laurels of what we've purchased. We need to move on to *how* we use what we've purchased.

The question should be, what is your carbon footprint? not what is the mpg rating of your car. For example, let's assume a green-thinking consumer buys a car with a 30-mpg rating, having shed her big SUV that only got 15 miles per gallon. That's great, but she should ask herself what her carbon footprint is before she wears even a scarf of self-righteousness. If someone drives 30,000 miles a year in a 30-mpg vehicle, she consumes 1,000 gallons of gas. If someone drives 6,000 miles a year in a 15-mpg vehicle, she consumes 400 gallons of gas. That means that, loosely speaking, the person who drives the less efficient vehicle has an automotive carbon footprint that is 40 percent of the person driving the more efficient vehicle farther. If a car is a transportation tool, the question is how one uses the tool.

A Toyota Prius, the current automotive poster child of the green set, generates about 3.4 tons of carbon emissions a year. This compares quite favorably to a Honda Accord, which generates 6 to 7.8 tons of carbon emissions a year, or a Dodge Ram truck at 9.7 to 12 tons per year. If the owner of the Prius drives three times as much as the owner of the Accord, then she is contributing more to global warming. Of course, it is better to drive a lower-mpg car, but the real question is, what is the carbon footprint of our behavior?

I have a car that I love to drive. It is a 12-year-old Mustang convertible, with a large V-8 engine that has 84,000 miles on the odometer. It's powerful and in relatively good shape. I haven't made a car payment in over six years. The problem is it gets an in-city mpg in the mid teens, so it is not a very fuel-efficient form of transportation. Therefore I have taken two steps to lessen my carbon footprint. The first step is to not drive a lot. I live in the city, work at home, and therefore put around 3,000 miles a year on the car. I walk around the neighborhood to do most of my errands, and I take public transportation a lot. My contribution to global warming is lessened by driving less. The second thing I've done is purchase carbon offsets to balance both my driving and the energy I use to live in my home. I purchased my offsets from Planktos (http://www.planktos.com) because I know the CEO and love the fact that the money goes to grow plankton blooms in the ocean.

So start to think about your activities in terms of your annual carbon footprint, your total contribution to global warming over a year. Thinking about this might lead you to purchase carbon offsets, so your entire lifestyle is carbon-neutral. It must be stated that carbon offsets should be looked at as a short-term solution until we all drive electric cars, consume only renewable energy, and have started to reverse global warming. The carbon offsets I purchased help to restore the oceans, so, while it makes me feel good about being carbon-neutral, it is also helping the earth by growing plankton in the oceans.

Another term to think about is "food miles," or the miles your food travels to get to the store where you purchase it. If you live in Chicago and like to think you are conscious because you eat organic food, you're not helping things if that organic food is flown in from California, as the emissions for that transport contribute to global warming. This is why there is such a growing movement to buy locally grown produce. Not only does it tend to be fresher, but it has not been transported over long distances using fossil fuels. Ask your store where the produce comes from.

So what is your carbon footprint? Have you purchased carbon offsets where the money you spend goes to help reforest the earth? How much of your life have you made carbon-neutral? How many food miles do you have in your refrigerator? New language can lead to new thinking, which can lead to new behavior.

• • •

Sputnik: 50 Years Later

October 3, 2007

It was 50 years ago this week that the Russians launched Sputnik, the first man-made satellite to orbit the earth. It changed the world. In fact, there are few, if any, events of the last 50 years that had such a global impact on just about every aspect of humanity.

I can still remember the night that, as a young boy standing in the front yard with my parents, I looked up at the starry sky waiting for Sputnik. There it was, a slow man-made star moving across the sky. We listened to its beeping on the radio. It filled me with wonder. I did not see it as Russian but rather as man-made; we humans had done this. "The sky's the limit" was a phrase of the past. This was space!

The launch of Sputnik caused great consternation in the United States. We had fallen behind the Russians. We were no longer the only player at the center of the stage of human dreams and aspirations. It has been universally acknowledged that this event triggered the space race and jump-started a decades-long emphasis on the teaching of science at all levels in the United States. In the context of the Cold War, this country felt threatened, vulnerable, and challenged. That history has been well documented, so I will look at other developments that flowed from this event 50 years ago that suggest how truly significant it really was.

Sputnik took space out of science fiction into reality, from "what if" to now. A man-made object had left the planet, lowering the perceived wall of limitation to show a field of unimaginable possibility. It became a reference point and a metaphor of potential as in, "Hey, if the Russians can put a satellite into space we can do _____." (Fill in the blank with whatever dream was being discussed.) It was this type of thinking that led to President Kennedy's great speech in 1961 about landing a man on the moon and bringing him home safely before the end of the decade. Thinking opened up.

The seeds of thinking globally were first strewn with Sputnik. When John Glenn and then others orbited the planet, the world listened as one to the human communications from space. We all watched it on TV. One of us, a human, was up there. Then there were two of us, then three at a time. Every launch into space became the dominant news story for the duration of the flight. It led the newscasts and was always on the front page. Eleven years after Sputnik, on Christmas Eve, 1968, the famous "earthrise" photo was broadcast from Apollo 8. We all saw the earth as a beautiful blue planet surrounded by infinite blackness. Our planetary home seemed so fragile and alone in the universe.

This was the first time in the history of humanity that we could all see a photograph of our planet from space. This single image, more than any other, launched the environmental movement. It was clear that the planet was precious and finite. The first Earth Day was in 1970, 13 years after the launch of Sputnik. In some long and winding way, our current global environmental consciousness has grown from the launch of Sputnik. Marshall McLuhan's great environmental quote was based in space terminology: "There are no passengers on planet earth. We are all crew."

The possibility of space, which we started to live with after Sputnik, helped to shape the tumultuous decade of the 1960s. While Vietnam, civil rights, rock music, and drugs are most often sourced as the change agents of this decade, space exploration was also a major influence. Astrology, a practice of prediction based on planets, became quite popular—Age of Aquarius, anyone? Thinking opened up. Equal rights? Why not! Make love not war? Yes! If man can go into space, he can solve terrestrial problems.

Sputnik also started something that was quite significant in the United States. In World War II, the country had been completely mobilized to win the Great War. What the country accomplished in those few short years had no historical precedence. After the war and up until Sputnik, the United States took a much-needed prosperity break. This was the time of television, suburbia, and the car culture. We had won, and we enjoyed the fruits of our winning. Sputnik triggered a mobilization in the country. America showed itself to be able to mobilize around a goal, a mission of great historical magnitude. In 12 short years we went from a small sphere beeping its way around the planet to actually walking on the moon. The government, NASA, business, and the citizenry all coalesced around this incredibly inspiring mission.

We need to do this again today. This time not just as a nation but as one of many nations that need to collaborate to solve the global energy problem. Now, as in 1957, we are threatened, vulnerable, and challenged; only now it is all of humanity who faces a massive problem. Today it is the challenge of finding completely renewable energy as fast as we can. Once again the solution is space. A number of the great scientists support an Apollo-like program to launch and build massive orbital solar space stations. Kilometers across, these massive solar panels in space can provide almost all the energy needs of humanity before the end of this century. Called space solar power (SSP) or space solar energy (SSE), it is the single best big solution for the planet.

All energy on earth comes directly or indirectly from the sun. The sun is the source of all energy in our solar system. By putting several large solar panels in geosynchronous orbit around the planet and transmitting the solar energy captured back down to earth, we can provide energy to earth for as long as there is the sun. The technology is available, and, during the course of the 20 years it will take to put the first SSP satellite in orbit, it can be further refined. The good news is that entrepreneurial space companies in the private sector are fast approaching the time when they can create a business of shuttling back and forth into space, delivering all the materials needed for these massive satellites. A true partnership of government direction and funding, supported by for-profit companies and a vision of hope, unity, and survival on the part of all global citizens.

It is clear that this goal needs to be set. The citizens of the world and their governments need to come together around another space-based vision that will not only solve the most pressing problem of the time but would also, through the effort, forge the beginning of a new global era of cooperation. Why not? Look what we did after Sputnik!

CHAPTER 7:
OUR AUTOMOTIVE FUTURE

W E LIVE WITH climate change, pollution, and a dwindling oil supply. But, despite steady improvement in other areas of technology in the last century, our automobiles remain almost entirely reliant on the outdated internal combustion engine and its thirst for petroleum.

The five columns in this chapter consider research-and-development efforts that could lead to clean transportation. "An Electric Car" and "A Man Who Wants to Change the World" focus on the General Motors commitment to its electric car, the Chevrolet Volt. "The Quest for the Perfect Battery: Part One" and "The Quest for the Perfect Battery: Part Two" examine the need for an affordable, durable battery to power electric cars that can compete in the market—and on the streets. "The Compressed Air Car" encourages us to look everywhere for the innovative ideas that can transform our automotive future into a clean, sustainable one.

An Electric Car

February 12, 2007

The good news from the Chicago Auto Show is the large companies clearly are embracing hybrid and electric cars and innovative technologies. Yes, there are the cool concept cars scattered around the floor, but I'm more interested in what will actually come to market.

Invited by General Motors to behind-the-scenes briefings, I went to the auto show to learn how GM is truly reacting to the global-warming reality. (While there are other companies working on hybrid and electric cars, GM is the one that contacted me, shared information with me, and discussed issues with me, which is why I focus on GM in this column and others.)

I was curious about the Chevrolet Volt. I had heard the hype about this electric car when it was revealed to the world at the Detroit Auto Show in January. The headline then was that GM would produce this battery-powered, four-passenger vehicle that uses a gas engine to create additional electricity to extend the driving range. The Volt can be fully charged by plugging it into a 110-volt outlet for six hours a day. A full charge can deliver up to 40 miles of driving in the city. This is a significant number because more than 50 percent of Americans live 20 miles or less from work. If the car were used just for commuting and errands in the neighborhood, it is possible, as Bob Lutz, GM vice chairman and automotive legend, said, "You might never burn a drop of gas during the life of the car."

I'm excited that GM is making its electric car under the Chevrolet name and not a new "tech" brand, as Chevrolet has long been the popular, mainstream GM brand. It sends the right message that this is to be a popular car for America.

The show model of the Volt is an extremely stylish and innovative car. I've always believed it's imperative for the alternative energy automotive business to create cars that are cool. We want to do the right thing, but we've grown up in a car-crazed culture and enjoy snazzy designs and cars that are fun to drive. If electric cars are, stylistically speaking, the automotive design equivalent of earth shoes, that will limit the number of cars sold. If, however, electric and hybrid cars can look and drive great, more people will buy them. And the goal, of course, is to get the largest percentage possible of global drivers to use such cars.

I asked the Volt design team how many of the incredibly cool design features, inside and out, will actually make it to the model that ultimately goes on sale. The team members hope as many as possible because they agree design should be a key selling point for the electric car. They did say GM asked them to be innovative and cutting-edge during the design process. While there are some elements that will likely not make it to the Volt that arrives at your dealer's showroom, it has such a cool quotient already that even a style-compromised, mass-production version should turn heads.

When will the Volt come to market, how much will it cost, and how many will GM produce? The answer to all three questions revolves around the battery. Right now there is no battery that exists that can satisfy the basic requirements of a mass-production vehicle that is also affordably priced. Lutz stated the metrics, "The battery must be able to last for 10 years, be able to sustain 5,000 charges, and not generate significant heat." When today's lithium ion batteries are connected together to generate enough power for a car, they create too much heat, and durability is called into question.

Troy Clarke, the GM vice president for North America, said the Volt will make it to market by the end of the decade. Surprised that it would take so long, given all the Volt's parts are already used in production on other vehicles, I pressed him on why it would take so long. He cited the unknowns around the battery: it's unclear how long it will take to develop a battery that can satisfy the needs and not price the Volt out of the mass market. When I asked Clarke if GM is fully committed to the Volt, he gave a firm yes, saying the marketplace has expressed strong interest in electric and hybrid cars, and GM wants to sell cars the market wants. GM already has numerous requests from individuals and companies for multiple Volts.

In an interview with Larry Burns, the vice president for Research & Development and Strategic Planning for GM, I asked whether the process to solve the battery issue would be slowed by a "not invented here" mindset, meaning GM would insist on internally developing the battery. He said GM has put out the message to key suppliers and partners that it's serious about bringing the Volt and other vehicles that use battery technology to market and asked for help to get GM there quickly and affordably.

There is existing battery technology that can be used in cars, but it is either limited or expensive. The EV1 battery technology of the 1990s didn't provide enough power and durability and wasn't cheap enough to be practical for the larger auto market. Tesla Motors is bringing out its incredibly fast, high-performance electric sports car—but at $100,000.

The reality of great numbers of us driving fun and affordable electric cars in the next five years is contingent on the invention of new batteries that can be durable, affordable, and mass-produced. GM and other companies, by their firm commitment to produce electric cars, have in effect created a future mass market. I believe that conservation technologies and alternative energy are the greatest economic opportunity in the history of humanity. Who wants to get rich?

I've heard several times the perhaps apocryphal story of Ray Bradbury, the great science fiction writer, who was asked for a short description of the history of entrepreneurship in the United States. After much deliberation, he came up with "the garage." Where are the Jobs and Wozniaks of the battery business?

• • •

A Man Who Wants to Change the World

February 15, 2007

Larry Burns is the vice president of Research & Development and Strategic Planning at GM. Simply put, this means he is *the* person responsible for leading GM into the future of clean transportation. It is Burns's job to initiate and oversee research, lead, innovate, prod, motivate, and, yes, seduce all those he comes in contact with to buy into a new vision of automotive transportation.

I interviewed Burns prior to the Chicago Auto Show to learn how committed GM is and will be to cleaner automobiles.

At the outset of our conversation, I made it clear that I was impressed with GM's commitment to the Chevrolet Volt and increasingly efficient and green vehicles. That said, I challenged him to show me what was on his drawing board that was more than just an aggregation of ways to increase overall fleet mpg by degrees and do enough green initiatives to satisfy the marketing department. I wanted to hear plans for transformation, not incremental change. I got what I asked for.

Burns wants to change the automotive world, simple as that. As our conversation went on, he revealed more and more of his passion for creating alternatives to the internal combustion engine; currently 98 percent of vehicles run on petroleum energy only, which does not make sense if we are going through peak oil. He said the future of vehicular power is blended fuel, electric batteries, and hydrogen and other fuel cells. He pulled out a PowerPoint presentation he'd made earlier in the day, and I found myself being educated on the possibilities that lie ahead.

Burns spoke animatedly about the Chevrolet Sequel and the Chevrolet Equinox Fuel Cell cars that GM is currently producing in very limited numbers—and at probably extremely high cost. I found I couldn't digest the information as fast as he was sharing it. At my request, Burns gave me a hand-labeled disk copy of his presentation. GM asked me to not show it to anyone but knew that I was going to write about my interview with Burns, so I will quote from it here, as it is as good a presentation on the world today as it relates to energy and the possible future of automotive transportation as I have ever seen. After an extensive setup on the state of energy in the world today, Burns provides some GM specifics:

> The Chevrolet Sequel is the most technologically advanced vehicle in the world. It is specifically designed around hydrogen fuel cell technology. The propulsion system combines GM's fourth-generation fuel cell with three electric motors and a lithium ion battery to give jet-like acceleration characteristics and all-wheel drive with side-to-side torque control.

> Project Driveway, a new test program, will put our latest fuel cell/electric vehicle—the Chevrolet Equinox Fuel Cell—into the hands of customers next year.... [I]ts technology is seamlessly integrated and has been fully engineered and tested to meet all existing government standards. General Motors is building 100 of these vehicles and will be placing them with customers later this year. Project Driveway constitutes the first meaningful market test of fuel cell/electric vehicles anywhere.

These slides were followed by a couple of incredible slides. Here are some highlights:

> By keeping our vehicles quite simple, storing hydrogen and electricity on board the vehicle, and using electric drive and fuel cells, we have the opportunity to use every energy pathway—from fossil fuels to renewable sources.

Our vehicles will emit zero emissions. And when the hydrogen and electricity is made from a renewable source, the entire system—from energy generation to torque at the wheels—will be zero-emissions.

This type of propulsion replaces complex gasoline, diesel, and hybrid systems with a single system that has only a tenth as many moving parts as a conventional power train system.

The design flexibility enabled by scalable fuel cells, electric batteries, and electronic controls will drive new vehicle designs and provide the potential to lower costs.

And, finally: "When you connect all the dots, this is truly a compelling opportunity to reinvent the automobile and the automobile business and accelerate industry growth in a sustainable way."

This guy works for General Motors. On top of that, he reports directly to the chairman, Rick Waggoner!

My interview with Burns was scheduled for 15 minutes. An hour later I walked out of our meeting excited, with a sense of transformation and real possibility. Not only had I met an incredibly intelligent man but one on a mission. If all of us who feel an urgency to get on with the job of slowing global warming and ending our insane dependency on petroleum could describe the person to have be in a true position of power at a major automobile company, it would be Burns.

The people I most like to spend time with are people who have, can, or want to change the world. My hope is that GM will have the long-range intelligence and commitment to let Larry Burns do just that.

• • •

The Quest for the Perfect Battery: Part One

March 16, 2007

One of the most important research-and-development efforts in the world today is the quest for the perfect battery to power electric cars. We know there global warming, air pollution, and an increasing dependence on imported oil exist. We know petroleum is a finite resource that will be depleted in this century. We live in a country whose culture is so dependent on the automobile that an alien might think the car is the dominant form of life. The solution is to reinvent how the more than 200 million vehicles in this country are powered.

It has been 120 years since the internal combustion engine was invented and first used for a mode of personal transportation. In that time, the 20th century, practically every technological aspect of our lives has been consistently upgraded, changed, or replaced by a new invention. Not so the power train of the automobile, which, at its essence, is still the mechanical, internal combustion engine we were using in 1900.

This then is the historical context in which the automotive industry and its suppliers are attempting to invent an electric power source for the vehicles we drive.

I met with some of the top management of General Motors last month, prior to the Chicago Auto Show. In follow-up, GM invited me to Detroit to attend both a breakfast meeting and a briefing on the status of the development of battery technology for the electric car.

While there are other automotive companies working on hybrid and electric cars, most notably Toyota and the yet-to-come-to-market Tesla, GM has opened itself up to me, so it is GM that I will write about in this ongoing series of columns on the automotive quest for the holy grail: a battery technology suitable for powering all our vehicles.

There were several events I attended during my 24 hours in Detroit. The major one was the battery briefing. GM assembled not only several of their top executives and engineers but also executives of the companies selected to help GM develop the battery technology needed first for the Chevrolet Volt and then for the rest of its product line. GM has selected two suppliers for advanced battery development. One is a joint venture between Johnson Controls and Saft, and the other is Cobasys, who will work in partnership with A123 Systems.

GM has chosen the lithium ion battery as the best technology to develop going forward. Current hybrids, such as the Prius, use nickel metal hydride batteries, which are not good enough for the plug-in concept of the Chevrolet Volt. Current hybrids use batteries to help power the car and the gasoline engine for greater mileage; the plug-in concept of the Volt uses a small gas engine to help recharge the battery, and it is the battery that powers the car. Since nickel metal batteries are not up to that task, the full force of the GM effort is to develop the lithium ion battery so it's suitable for a mass-production vehicle.

What is needed is a battery pack that lasts for 5,000 charges, lasts for 100,000 miles, powers the car for at least 40 miles on a charge, can be mass-produced at low prices, is completely reliable, and does not overheat. No battery pack currently meets these criteria. Lithium ion batteries power the laptops we use, and we have all read about the combustibility problem there. Powering up a car and driving it 60 miles an hour, in temperatures that range from below 0 to over 100 degrees Fahrenheit, is an entirely different task than powering up a laptop. Tesla is coming up with a battery pack, but the price of the auto is $100,000, in large part due to the high cost of the battery. GM is a mass-production company, so it needs a battery that can be manufactured in large quantities at low costs. If the electric car is to become transformative, the masses must be able to buy reliable, affordable, long-lasting electric cars that cost the same as gasoline-powered cars. Otherwise, it will be a technology available only to the rich and will have limited global effect.

The questions to the executives at the battery briefing pointed out two dominant lines of questioning. The first is obvious to anyone who saw *Who Killed the Electric Car?* and that is to openly doubt the commitment of GM to follow through on its claims to want to reinvent the automobile. The second is to call into question the position that GM has taken that it will not bring out an electric car until a perfect battery pack has been developed. In other words, why wait until 2010—the stated expected launch year for the Volt—to deliver an electric car that, though not perfect, could be used by a number of drivers in this country to start to solve global warming, air pollution, and our dependence on imported oil?

• • •

The Quest for the Perfect Battery: Part Two

March 20, 2007

Is General Motors for real? All evidence points to a truly serious, committed company that has set as one of its core missions to reinvent the actual DNA of the automobile. First, GM is being extremely open with the press, bloggers, and the world at large about what it's doing, with whom, what the goals are, and what the problems are in reaching those goals. This is not one of those secret skunk works that companies set up to develop product X. The announcement of the Chevrolet Volt in January was accompanied by announcements that GM had selected three partners—A123, Cobasys, and a joint venture of Johnson Controls and Saft—to work with it on the quest for the perfect battery.

During the briefing I was invited to attend in Detroit last week, GM executives went first, followed by a senior executive from each partner. After their presentations, the executives were subjected to any and all questions from the assembled group of media representatives. I personally found conversations with Scott Lindholm from Cobasys and Ed Bednarcik of A123 to be very honest, informative, and exciting. Not once did I feel I was fed a line or subjected to convenient spin.

The thrust of the entire exercise last week was a stated openness. GM is going to let us know every step of the way what is going on and who is responsible for what; the process is open and as transparent as a huge corporation can make it. GM is basically saying, "We don't yet have the solution, but here is what we are going to do, and, as things develop, we will share that progress." Perhaps other major auto companies are doing that, but I am not aware of them at this date. Dueling press releases are nothing more than that. Openness about the process is to be applauded.

The ones I know who doubt GM's intentions are hard-core environmentalists who have developed good reason to doubt green claims from big business. The answers to them and everyone are clear and business-obvious. First, there is a very strong demand for green cars, and GM is in the business of selling into demand, selling people what they want. Second, almost all vehicles being produced are powered by petroleum, and petroleum is a declining resource. Whether the world runs out of petroleum in 30 years or 60 years, run out we will, so why would any company want to have long-term plans to produce transportation vehicles that can't transport?

The second question—why not come out with a short-term-fix vehicle that will satisfy the clear and strong demand for a low-emission, electric car?—is a slightly more complex one. I had come into the briefing with that exact concern. From a marketing point of view, in this evermore green marketplace, why not give the people what they want and score major points in the process? Why wait when something can be done now? The simple answer from GM is that anything that does not meet the demanding criteria of the buying public, green or otherwise, is not worth doing, as it will ultimately be doomed to failure or be an extremely contained success at best. Remember, the name of the car is the Chevrolet Volt. GM is putting its number one brand name on it, the brand name for Middle America. GM has taken a stand with its core brand, not some "tech" brand that is at arm's length.

This was again brought home by an intimate breakfast with Larry Burns, the vice president of Research & Development and Strategic Planning for GM. I've described Burns as a man who wants to change the world, and I believe he does. It is almost his job description. Burns gave me and the three others in attendance a presentation on GM's plans for the future.

It was at first disorienting and then exhilarating. The briefing took place in a boardroom at GM's R&D Center, a big, sprawling complex that, since I love modern, mid-century architecture, I found extremely beautiful. So here we were, sitting at the heart of GM being told by a top executive that "the time for energy diversity is now," that "98 percent of energy used to power cars is from petroleum," that with current developments "a new DNA of the automobile is emerging," and that this new DNA will exchange the internal combustion engine for electric propulsion, petroleum for electricity and hydrogen, and mechanical systems for electric and electronic systems.

Burns, in most emphatic terms, said it is time "to reinvent the automobile." That is what he sees as his job. His passion, knowledge, and commitment are real. And, folks, he is the guy leading the way at GM. He is telling anyone who will listen that this is his job. His presentation, by the way, is one of the most cohesive, comprehensive, and informative presentations I have ever seen on what is going on in the world, on what the automotive industry is doing in this context, and, of course, on all the specifics of what GM has, is, and will be doing.

When I asked him why the company is not putting out stopgap, short-term solutions in the form of cars that use current technology, his answer was powerful in its simplicity. He said, "Why? It wouldn't really solve the problem. The only solution is to sell massive amounts of vehicles for there to be any impact, and the only way to do so is to find a battery technology that can be produced cheaply enough to be affordable to millions, that is safe and reliable, and that can perform at levels as good as and probably better than the internal combustion options currently available to people." OK, right answer.

I expect subsequent chapters in this "Quest for the Perfect Battery" series, as I find it one of the most important R&D efforts currently going on in the world. Thanks to GM, I have had a front row seat so far and hope to continue to report from that vantage point.

• • •

The Compressed Air Car

July 17, 2007

It is important to realize that the way we power our vehicles today is based on the legacy of energy discoveries of the 1800s. Oil was first taken out of the ground in Pennsylvania in the 1860s. When the automobile industry came into being some four decades later, petroleum was the first candidate for the energy source. Even though the quintessential American inventor Thomas Edison did build an electric car, electricity was not as wide spread as it soon would be, so the power of the Rockefeller oil cartel won the day.

Today we are using the energy source discovered 150 years ago to get us to work and to the grocery store. Do we use candles to light our homes? Do we use tubes to power our radios and TVs? Do we cool our houses with blocks of ice? No, no, and no! So why do we continue to blindly define transportation energy on a 150-year-old discovery that we know causes climate change, funds terrorism, and is in finite supply?

In the last few decades, Western science, as it has penetrated ever-smaller particles, has concluded that everything is energy. From this point of view, it strikes me as incredibly narrow to think of energy as fossil fuel. Fossil fuel is just a small slice of what is available. If everything is energy, then let's look elsewhere, everywhere.

There are people around the world who are doing just that. The French company MDI has partnered with the Indian company Tata Motors to bring to market a car that runs on compressed air. That's right: air. The power source is air, and the waste product is air. A visionary inventor and entrepreneur, Guy Nègre, the founder of MDI, has developed a compressed air engine that has the potential for being one of the great inventions of this century.

Nègre's compressed air car can travel 120 to 175 miles between refueling. That is significant because more than 50 percent of Americans live 20 miles or less from work, and the average daily mileage per car is less than 40 miles. The cost to operate is low, about $1 per hundred miles. The car will need to go to compressed air fueling stations for a refill. Once these retrofitted gas stations are in place, a refueling will take three minutes, will cost about $2, and will allow the driver to drive 120 to 175 miles.

Alternatively, there are engines being developed that switch to either electric or gas power, allowing the car to be driven while at the same time operating the compressor to refill the tank with compressed air. This model car could be driven from Los Angeles to New York on a single tank of gas. Because there is no heat-generating combustion in the engine, changing the oil—vegetable oil at that—needs to be done only once every 30,000 miles.

What is not to like about cars that are pollution-free, basically petroleum-free, low-cost to purchase (estimates are less than $20,000), low-cost to operate, and capable of handling most of our driving needs? Sure, if you want to pull a boat or rumble around in a big SUV or pickup, this vehicle is not for you, but for commuting and running errands, the overwhelming amount of vehicular use in the United States, the compressed air car is just fine.

The compressed air car points to the fact that humanity has the technological capability of solving our energy problems in transportation. Combined with the coming electric cars, it is possible that by 2020 we could primarily be free of our reliance on the internal combustion engine. That is the potential and clear possibility. Do we have the social and political fortitude to make this a reality? Will our government see the clear opportunity, or will it succumb to historical habit and inertia and cave to the well-funded industry lobbying efforts that have influenced energy and transportation policy for the last 100 years?

The presidential candidates in 2008 could campaign on an "Energy Independence by 2015" platform, calling for government-supported mass production of electric cars and compressed air cars and creating a nationwide Apollo project for the replacement of the internal combustion engine in a decade. The technology is soon to be in place, so it is up to us, all of us, to use the compressed air car and all such emerging new technologies to make it a reality.[1]

CHAPTER 8:
A TIME OF DISINTERMEDIATION

Y OU PROBABLY HAVEN'T heard the term *disintermediation* bandied about much since the late 1990s, but the disintermediating impact of the Internet is a defining force of our times.

Reviving the term, the columns in this chapter examine disintermediation in the early 21st century. "Disintermediation: A Buzzword to Bring Back" and "Disintermediation: A Deeper Look" establish a definition for and general characteristics of disintermediation today. The remaining five columns—"Watching Video, Selling a Home, Buying Insurance"; "The Political Party in the United States: A Candidate for Disintermediation?"; "Guilty Pleasures"; "Disintermediation Is Rarely Partial"; and "Say Good-bye to the 6-percent Commission Rule"—look at the role disintermediation plays in media, real estate, insurance, and politics.

Disintermediation: A Buzzword to Bring Back

April 14, 2006

Disintermediation was a buzzword in the late 1990s when Internet 1.0 was filling people with euphoria about how the world would change.

Internet evangelists were saying that the Web would largely eliminate the transactional middleman. This clearly came to pass in the travel industry as people researched and booked travel directly online, doing a lot of comparison price shopping along the way. This, to a large degree, eliminated the travel agent, the middleman in this case, from the equation. When airlines saw this trend and cancelled the fee they traditionally paid travel agents, the game changed forever. I'll bet the growth of Starbucks was fueled in part by all the former travel agents becoming baristas.

The other market space that underwent disintermediation was the stockbrokerage business. People could buy and sell stock online; no phone calls to brokers were needed. The concept, practice, and profession of day-trading came into being. Transactions became almost immediate. Research was available online. Transaction fees plummeted. Who needed some broker talking to them on the phone and charging them commissions that greatly limited trading profit potential? As the coffee business swelled with well-traveled baristas, the ranks of independent financial advisors swelled with former stockbrokers using their country club memberships to sell financial planning instead of hot stock tips.

Lately I haven't heard *disintermediation* much. Other buzzwords and phrases seem to have superseded it. However, as a futurist, as someone who looks at the present from the filter of the future and finds developing patterns, I think the word *disintermediation* needs to be reenergized. I see it going on everywhere, but I also see a larger historical context at play here.

First, a look at the dictionary as the usage that has developed is slightly different than the formal dictionary definition. *Merriam-Webster Online Dictionary* (http://www.m-w.com) defines *disintermediation* foremost as "the diversion of savings from accounts with low fixed interest rates to direct investment in high-yielding instruments." That must be a surprise to all those former Internet 1.0 evangelists.

However, *intermediate* is defined as "being or occurring at the middle place, stage, or degree or between extremes," and *intermediation* as "the act of coming between."

When I use the word *disintermediation*, I mean "the undoing of the act of intermediating; the removal of the intermediary person or entity."

The Internet, particularly in its current high-speed, broadband iteration, Internet 2.0, is the single most powerful agent of disintermediation there is at this time on earth. It is being used to change economic transaction structures in practically all areas of commerce. It is forcing heretofore firmly entrenched distribution channels to adapt or suffer significant negative consequences. It is the visible disintermediating agent for big economic, political, and cultural institutions in the United States and around the world.

We live in a special era of history that is, in a sense, a time of disintermediation, and the Internet is the primary invention/tool/agent of this age. There have been other times in humanity's recent history when, during a relatively short span of 50 to 60 years, the world reorganized to such a degree that it was a fundamentally different place at the end of the era than at the beginning. These eras always have a single dominant agent of disintermediation that not only breaks things up but also greatly accelerates the changes of the era.

In 1455 Johannes Gutenberg invented the moveable-type printing press, which became the primary agent of disintermediation of that time. Decades earlier Europe was in the Middle Ages; decades later the Renaissance flourished and was soon followed by the Reformation. Prior to Gutenberg's invention, written knowledge was largely held by the Catholic Church and royalty. In the century that followed, knowledge, disseminated via printed books, reached far beyond this most narrow of elites. This brought about a rapid expansion of education, philosophy, and scientific inquiry. Copernicus and Machiavelli wrote—and published—their great works in the early 1500s. There were other forces at play that helped move Europe from the Middle Ages to and through the Renaissance, but the moveable-type printing press was the primary agent of disintermediation.

Three hundred years later the invention of the steam engine had a similar effect. While there is some dispute as to whether Thomas Newcomen, who built the first steam engine in 1712, or James Watt, who received the first patent for the commercial use of the steam engine in 1769, was the inventor, there is no dispute that this invention was the change agent that began the transformation of the world from the Agricultural Age to the Industrial Age. In the 50 years from 1770 to 1820, capitalism, communism, democracy, and the Industrial Revolution were born. Clearly there were other forces at play, but it can certainly be argued that the steam engine was the dominant agent of disintermediation.

The point of this short historical discourse is to show that in key transformative periods in human history there is something that provokes, stimulates, and facilitates radical change in a relatively short time. Thanks in large part to Gutenberg's invention, the people who were alive in Europe in 1450 would not recognize the world their grandchildren lived in. The people alive in 1760 would not recognize the world their grandchildren lived in. As a baby boomer, I can most certainly say that the world my son will live in as an adult would have been extremely difficult for his grandparents to comprehend.

We now live in one of these occasional transformative periods when the world gets reordered. I sense that it has another 20 years to go. I use the name "Threshold Decades" for the 20-year period from 1985 to 2005. Think back to 1985 and how different the world is now than then. There was a Soviet Union; no global economy; no wide use of cell phones, Internet, or wireless devices; music on vinyl records or analog cassettes, not CDs or MP3s. My flash drive has more storage than the office PC of 1985. The list goes on. When Internet usage took off in the late 1990s and was again accelerated with the rapid expansion of bandwidth during the last four years, the speed of change and of disintermediation accelerated. The 20 years between now and 2026 will contain a much greater amount of transformative change than the past 20 years; of that I have no doubt.

The Internet, related technologies, and certain dynamic flows of history will cause or bring disintermediation to some degree to practically every part of our lives in the next two to three decades. We live in an era of disintermediation. So it is a buzzword I am bringing back because it describes the world in which we live. Use the word and embrace, or at least accept, the reality it describes.

• • •

Disintermediation: A Deeper Look

May 11, 2006

As I've defined it in an earlier column, *disintermediation* is "the undoing of the act of intermediating; the removal of the intermediary person or entity."

During the Internet 1.0 time of the late 1990s the travel industry and the stockbrokerage industry began to experience disintermediation. Thousands of travel agents and stockbrokers were put out of business as the Internet gave people direct access to necessary travel and stock information and gave them the ability to transact online. Of course, there are still travel agents and stockbrokers, but they no longer hold the same power or command the same income per transaction as they used to.

This brings me to the first point of this column: disintermediation does not necessarily wipe out a certain business, but it does drain it of excess compensation to the middleman.

Today we can chose to use a travel agent or chose to use a stockbroker; we no longer have to, and, if we do, it is at a lower cost than 10 years ago.

I always buy my airline tickets online because the information I need is available to me, the airlines usually make it the cheapest alternative, and it doesn't take much time. I'm planning a summer trip to Europe with my son right now, and I'm using a travel agent. Why? Because he will save me time. It would take me tens of hours to study German flight and train schedules, research hotels, and communicate with car rental agencies. Instead, I expect to spend perhaps two or three hours on the phone with my agent. I save time. He provides me with information learned from prior customers, so I have a knowledge base working for me. He has already found low-cost flights within Germany that I most likely would not have found. He has saved me money that will go against any commissions that may be on my side of the ledger. This is what a service economy is about: providing a service that saves me time and provides me with the opportunity for educated choice.

Historically, middlemen, or intermediaries, have been paid because they possess knowledge their clients don't have. Proprietary databases that only the middlemen have access to allow them to trade and act on that knowledge in return for rich fees. Knowledge is power. However, the Internet is the greatest agent of knowledge and information dissemination since Gutenberg's invention.

This leads me to the second point of this column: industries that try to hold information and knowledge hostage for financial benefit will ultimately succumb to disintermediation.

Withholding information is a losing proposition when thousands of terabytes course through the global Internet hourly. I have more information at my fingertips due to high-speed Internet and search engines than the greatest scholar did 20 years ago. I can find information faster than the world's best research librarian of the 1980s.

This leads me to the third point of this column: technology, in this era of the Internet, acts as an agent of disintermediation to existing distribution channels.

If there has been value ascribed to the distribution beyond the value of the content that it delivers, it will be drained away, as content or customers have the option of the Internet for distribution. Media is clearly the prime example here. Think of newspapers charging a subscription or newsstand price for the paper delivery of the news. Today you can receive the newspaper online without paying for the physical newspaper, so you get the same content but are no longer paying for the means of distribution.

In summary:

1. Disintermediation is the removal of the intermediary person or entity.
2. If the intermediary remains in place, it will be drained of any excess compensation.
3. Industries that hold information hostage for financial gain will be disintermediated.
4. The Internet will be the agent of disintermediation of existing distribution channels.

Next we will look at some of the industries that are undergoing disintermediation. Media is living it, real estate feels threatened, and insurance might not yet see it.

• • •

Watching Video, Selling a Home, Buying Insurance

May 17, 2006

In the last column on disintermediation, I gave a deeper current definition and meaning to the term:

1. Disintermediation is the removal of the intermediary person or entity.
2. If the intermediary remains in place, it will be drained of any excess compensation.
3. Industries that hold information hostage for financial gain will be disintermediated.
4. The Internet can be the agent of disintermediation of existing distribution channels.

We are living in a 50- to 60-year era of transformative change. Disintermediation is part of that transformation, as it always is in such eras. The most powerful agent of disintermediation today is the Internet, and it is affecting most industries. With the above definitions in mind, I want to look at some industries that have undergone, are undergoing, or are about to undergo disintermediation: media, real estate, and insurance.

Media has been living in a world of transformation and disintermediation for years. The basic power shift over the past 30 years has been from the supplier (network, station, newspaper) to the customer (viewer, listener, reader).

In the 1970s three networks controlled 90 percent of primetime TV viewing. There were three people who determined what Americans watched and when they watched it. These three people, usually middle-aged white men, were the heads of programming of ABC, CBS, and NBC, and they all worked in midtown Manhattan within blocks of each other. Now, 30 years later, there are 100+ networks, with 100+ heads of programming, of all ages and races, providing TV viewers with an incredibly diverse array of programming. That is just TV.

Video on the Internet has exploded during the past two years with the rapid growth of broadband. Now there are literally thousands of videos posted every day on the Internet, including an increasing number from the TV networks. That's why I used the word *video* in the title of this column. Video used to be delivered solely by television networks, so video equaled television. Now, thanks to the Internet, video has been separated from the TV set; there has been disintermediation.

What were the transformative, disruptive, and disintermediating technologies that changed and are continuing to change the video landscape?

- The remote control, which gives viewers perceived and actual control over what they watch
- Cable television, which dramatically increases the number of channels and which created the concept of targeted programming for targeted audiences, not just mass programming for mass audiences
- VCR and DVR technologies, which allow viewers to both watch when they want to watch and to fast-forward through commercials
- Broadband Internet, which allows video and programs to be viewed and downloaded to a computer or other electronic device

Radio has not been disintermediated as much as it has been overwhelmed by choice. Terrestrial radio has been joined by satellite radio, Internet radio, and podcasts. In addition, with tens of millions of MP3 players in the United States, there is a wealth of alternative ways to be entertained auditorily.

Newspapers are being disintermediated by the Internet. Classified advertising has gone to the Web, readership has gone to the Web, and the dead-tree physical distribution system of newspapers is being supplanted every day by the free and environmentally friendly distribution of the Internet. I personally believe that there will be a few national newspapers and that small town and small city newspapers will survive. The question is whether the mid- to large-sized city dailies can operate with increasing efficiency, adapting to the new landscape to find ways to survive, be relevant, and be businesses worth keeping alive. Have you noticed how often blogs and bloggers are cited in newspapers? Bloggers have become the new stringers of the newspaper business, supplanting the reporters who have been downsized out of jobs.

Magazines are currently being threatened by special-interest Web sites and by special-interest blogs. Magazines will undergo a market reorganization during a rough economic period in the next decade. Cost structures and paper costs will have to be addressed if this medium is to fend off disintermediation by the Internet. If people now read newspapers online, why will they not read magazines online? Fortunately for magazines and all print media, the advertisers will move online with them.

As the patron saint of media, Marshall McLuhan, said, "The medium is the message." The message of the Internet is always available, available anywhere, unlimited choice, and free. Go back to the top of this column and look at the four definitions of disintermediation; they all apply to media.

Now let's look at two other industries that are on the threshold of some degree of disintermediation. Using the four-part definition of the phenomenon, it is clear that real estate and insurance are going to be reorganized from historically developed structures based on transactions, fees, and processes.

I'm going to concentrate on residential real estate in this column because close to 70 percent of American families own their own homes. A much lower percentage of Americans have experience in commercial real estate. Since all real estate is local, there will be exceptions to the following generalizations, but, speaking broadly, these points hold true:

- Real estate agents have resisted changing their commission structure.
- Historically, these agents have tried to keep listing data to themselves.
- There is now an incredible amount of real estate price information on the Internet, and it is very easy to use the Internet to market a property to a potentially global customer base.

- In the last few years, there has been a dramatic increase in the number of for-sale-by-owner, or FSBO, listings, due in part to a heated real estate market, where the perception is that, if one puts a good property on the market, it will sell whether an agent is involved or not. The Internet supports this FSBO effort.

- Agent compensation doesn't seem to be tied to performance as much as tied to the past. This always is deadly in a service business, as people increasingly will look for the best value in a service relationship. This is a point that Stephen Dubner and Steven Levitt make in their wonderful book *Freakonomics*. (My readers know that these two have had kind words for my blog and that I think highly of their book—a must-read if you haven't already enjoyed it.)

If you're a real estate agent, please don't think I'm criticizing you. I am not, but take this as a friendly warning that, if you are not open to finding new ways of charging for your services, the market will soon start to dictate how you will be allowed to charge. Information empowers people, and all of the above points to a situation begging for disintermediation. Adapt now, and stay ahead of the curve, or hold on to "the way we've always done it" at your true peril. Here are some things to consider:

- Always remember you are providing a service to your client; bring value such as the saving of time, which saves money. People will pay to have the "heavy lifting" done for them. People pay for that and for good financial results; provide both.

- Be willing to come up with innovative commission deals, so that, if you do a good job, you will make more than if you just do an acceptable job. An example would be to accept a lower commission on the listing price—say 4 percent—but take 20 percent of the price over the listing price. If a seller needs to sell quickly, build in a bonus if the property sells fast. Now all of this can be manipulated around the listing price, but the buyer will think more kindly and supportively about your efforts as your self-interest and theirs align. Mutually agree to a fee with the seller. Good brokers will make more money; bad brokers will make less money. If you're good, don't be scared: show how good you are, and you will have your choice of clients.

- Remember that disintermediation removes *excess* compensation for intermediaries. That means that either fees will come down for the same job or will stay the same for a superior job where value has been added. Become a discount real estate broker, or add a new, higher level of service and a customized fee structure. As an agent you have a choice.

If you watch TV you will have inevitably seen a commercial from an insurance company asking you to call or go online for a quote that will save you money. This is direct marketing from the company to the consumer, cutting out the cost of paying an agent's commission. This is a clear example of disintermediation. Why do you think the other type of insurance commercial is all about the agent being helpful to the customer? Because that is the only value left. Twenty years ago the only way to learn about insurance was to meet with an agent; now all the information you need is online.

In the last century, each community had an insurance agent who provided a service and information, and everyone went to him; it was the only place to go. Today, if agents don't provide some true added service value, they will wonder where their commissions went, as everyone can buy insurance directly from the companies. The days of simply sending out renewal notices without providing any added value will soon be over. Canned newsletters and refrigerator magnets are not added value.

In a fear-based industry where life insurance is about death, auto insurance is about accidents, and homeowners insurance is about fire and theft, it is time to be real and help customers get the lowest price—or they will get it themselves. When the real estate companies believe they can create a direct relationship with the customer without an agent, the agent goes away, accepts a lower commission, or provides a personal service of some value beyond information about products.

In summary, much disintermediation has occurred in media, and the real estate and insurance industries are two obviously ripe areas to follow. There are a number of other areas that will be disintermediated to some greater or lesser degree. Just look to the four definitions and meanings stated in this column to remind you where disintermediation will occur.

• • •

The Political Party in the United States: A Candidate for Disintermediation?

May 31, 2006

In 1831 the national nominating convention started to replace the congressional caucus method of choosing nominees for the office of president of the United States. The delegates to the early conventions were either appointed by a party leader or were chosen under a party caucus system. This system remained in place until the early 1900s when the primary was introduced. The first primary to be used as a means of selecting delegates to the presidential nominating conventions took place in Florida in 1904. By 1916 20 Democratic and Republican state parties selected delegates using the primary system.

Even though primaries were introduced, they did not attract many voters, and the nominating process for both parties continued to be controlled by politicians in smoke-filled rooms who made deals and brokered candidates. The number of state primaries for both parties in which delegates were chosen stayed at 14 until the 1950s. Even though President Kennedy demonstrated electability by winning primaries, he won the convention nomination in 1960 by working the back rooms where the key party leaders agreed to support his candidacy.

In 1968 the upheaval at the Chicago convention lead to a reform movement that emphasized the primary system as a way to make the process of selecting a candidate more democratic, controlled by voters, not politicians. In 1968 37.5 percent of Democratic delegates and 34.3 percent of Republican delegates were selected by the primary system. By 1976 those figures were 72.6 percent and 67.9 percent, respectively. These percentages continued to increase to 2000, when 85.7 percent of Democratic delegates and 93.1 percent of Republican delegates were selected by primaries. In the last 30 years of the 20th century the power to select the party presidential nominee moved from politicians making deals in back rooms to voters at the polls in the primaries.

The other significant influence on the party convention institution was the addition of broadcast coverage. The first radio broadcast was in 1924. The first TV broadcast was in 1948. The TV coverage grew steadily through the 1950s, 1960s, 1970s, and 1980s, both in terms of the amount of coverage and the number of media outlets that covered it. Even local TV stations sent reporters to cover their community's angle. The conventions become staged-for-TV events, platforms to display the party candidates to the voters watching on TV.

Since the 1990s coverage of the conventions has shriveled, in large part because the conventions were no longer news stories but increasingly political party messaging mediums, and the networks didn't want to expend great resources on non-events. In the past two presidential election years, the broadcast networks didn't even devote three hours of prime time coverage, let alone the gavel-to-gavel coverage of prior years.

In the 1800s there were conventions that went on for days, with a large number of ballots, where political party leaders brokered nonstop to find acceptable nominees. The party added true value as they completely controlled the process. Even in the early 1900s there were, particularly on the Democratic side, conventions that had multiple ballots. There were 46 ballots in 1912, 44 in 1920, and even 103 in 1924. However, the last time it took more than one ballot to nominate a candidate was in 1948 on the Republican side (three ballots) and in 1952 on the Democratic side (also three ballots). Since 1956 every single Republican and Democratic nominee has won the first ballot. Simply put, the value of the politicians, those who used to control the back rooms, has been eliminated due to the primary system and the glare of the media.

What do we hear today about the two parties and what they stand for? Republicans who joined the party because of its commitment to fiscal restraint and smaller government say things like, "What happened to the Republican party that I joined years ago?" Democrats look around and say, "Where is the leadership of the Democratic party?" In other words, what happened to the political parties? Republicans are fighting wars of intervention and spending for big government; Democrats don't have an idea what they stand for.

Sounds like American political parties no longer serve any real purpose. They aren't really needed to provide the electorate with candidates. They don't really stand for anything. Polls show that the electorate feels the country, led by the two parties in all aspects of government, is going in the wrong direction, so the parties aren't providing leadership either. The political party, as currently defined in America, feels like an out-of-date, anachronistic apparatus whose value is in the past, not the present, and certainly isn't aligned with the future. If it is to survive, it must reconstitute itself, or it will crumble under its own dead weight.

We are in the middle of a 50- to 60-year transformation, one of those times that come along every few centuries when society is fundamentally reorganized. Institutions that had importance coming into such an age get relegated to the trash cans of history by the end of the era. Each of these recent ages had a force of disintermediation that was of the times: Gutenberg's moveable-type printing press in the 1400s, the invention of the steam engine in the 1700s, and now the Internet. How might this current age of transformation and the Internet change the institution of the American political party, either by replacing it or reinventing it?

. . .

Guilty Pleasures

September 6, 2006

I believe disintermediation is a fundamental force of reorganization in the world today. We live in an era of disintermediation.

We all have our guilty pleasures in life. The trashy shows on TV that we watch but don't really talk about, the Internet sites that we go to in private moments of mindless fun, the celebrity-packed magazines that fill us up with the seemingly glamorous lives of celebrities.

The other day I was checking out my RSS feeds, and I saw a post titled "Jimmy Page at 14." (This was on a site that usually has good, issue-oriented entries.) All my life I've been a Led Zeppelin fan, and I consider Jimmy Page one of the five great guitarists of the 1960s. To be able to see him at age 14! I immediately clicked the link, which took me to YouTube ultimately, where I watched a clip from a 1957 BBC program with "James Page" playing in a skiffle band and, during a break between songs, telling the interviewer that, when he grew up, he wanted to be a researcher to help solve cancer "if it hadn't been solved by then." This clip was grouped with other clips related to Led Zeppelin: Aerosmith playing with Led Zeppelin, Plant and Page playing in Brazil, and several Yardbirds clips. (For those of you who like rock-and-roll guitar, the Yardbirds had more guitar talent go through the lead guitar position than any other band in history. The first lead guitarist was Eric Clapton, the second was Jeff Beck, and the third and final was Jimmy Page.) All of these were clips I had never seen, never knew existed before, and thoroughly enjoyed. Well, 20 minutes later I finally went back to work with "Train Kept A-Rollin'" playing in my head. Thank you, YouTube, for a really nice, cool interlude.

YouTube is a poster child of disintermediation. It is less than a year old, and, in that short time, along with other sites such as IFILM, it has fundamentally altered the video and television landscape. Now videos break on YouTube then move to television. Want to be a star? Send your video to YouTube, and let the people decide, no programming executive needed.

So what does this have to do with disintermediation? Well, without going to a music store, a video rental store, a library, or a club, I got to watch great historic musical performances. I didn't have to pay anything, I didn't have to leave home, and I didn't need to buy anything, like a newspaper, to get the information about these clips. I found that information on a blog, supplied by a reader of that blog. So the entire experience, from beginning to end, was user-generated and -supplied, not media-outlet-generated; was free; and was completely convenient. There was no middleman telling when I had to watch, how much I had to pay, or in what order I had to watch what I wanted to watch.

It is 49 years since a 14-year-old Page made that remark about working on a cure for cancer when he grew up if it hadn't yet been solved. Well, we still have to finish that incredibly important task and as fast as possible. However, we do have some of the greatest rock and roll to listen to while we do it. Maybe, just maybe, the person responsible for the next great cancer breakthrough will cite "Stairway to Heaven" as an inspiration.

• • •

Disintermediation Is Rarely Partial

March 28, 2007

The CD business has been in decline ever since Napster came on the scene in the late 1990s. The industry became alarmed that sales first stopped increasing on a unit basis. When companies arrogantly increased prices without adding value to stem the decline, sales declined further. Then, oblivious to the winds of disintermediation starting to blow through their industry, they actually started to sue customers. (It's clear an industry has no clue when it initiates legal action against its customer base). All of this was done when sales were decreasing annually by single digits. Sales had historically always gone up, so a drop of 5 to 10 percent a year was both unheard of and terrifying.

Well, last week it was announced that on a year-to-year basis, sales of CDs were down 20 percent for the first three months of 2007. Not 5 percent, not 10 percent, but a full 20 percent! Those are numbers of an industry that is truly in decline and in the process of being fully disintermediated. CDs still account for 85 percent of all music sold, but the sharp slide this year is far greater than the growth in sales of digital downloads. Legal download sites such as iTunes are generating substantial revenue but come nowhere close to offsetting the declining sales of CDs. Music can be downloaded from illegal sites or from MySpace pages or MP3 blogs. In addition, many music stores have closed. In just the last year, more than 800 music stores, including 89 Tower Record stores, have closed. The old distribution system is shutting down. The experience of going into a store to get a CD and walking out with two or three bought on impulse is an ever-rarer experience.

When an industry gets disintermediated, the basic product model falls apart. Since the days of the 1960s and such seminal theme albums as *Sergeant Pepper*, music has been sold as albums. What that usually meant was that you bought a product that had two or three great songs and six to nine songs that were filler. With digital downloading, the music business has increasingly become a business of singles. The album model is falling away. The phrase that comes to mind is "cherry-picking": get what you want, and leave the rest behind.

In the 1950s the music business was built on singles. When albums became the product, industry revenues exploded. Due to disintermediation, we're now going back to the singles model. In the 1950s an artist was sent out on tour to build demand for the record, which was the product. Now managers of music groups look at the CD as the promotional vehicle for the tour, which is the product. Attending a concert and hearing music live is not an experience that can be disintermediated, so it has become the product again.

All this has happened at a time when it seems that people are listening to more music than ever. On the way to work, while working, while working out, while walking to class or down the street, people everywhere have earpieces that deliver self-selected soundtracks. The demand for music is stronger than ever, but the structures of the music business are collapsing. That is a definition of disintermediation.

• • •

Say Good-bye to the 6-percent Commission Rule

June 26, 2007

In the last year I have written often about disintermediation. It is a force affecting numerous industries. Residential real estate is one of those businesses. Any business that has historically inserted itself between buyer and seller and has also kept market information to itself is a business that sooner or later will have to redefine itself in this Internet age. Both the stockbrokerage and travel agent business have changed substantially due to the disintermediating power of the Internet. I predicted last year that residential real estate would soon be facing a similar situation unless it adapted quickly.

My recommendation has been for residential real estate agents to either lower their commission from the standard 6 percent or add services and create new value to keep their commission at that level. I want to be very clear: I'm not arguing against the status quo of this industry; I'm just saying that the trend is obvious and relentless and should be fully faced. The old days are over. Agents who do not believe this do so at their peril.

It has been no surprise to me to see numerous articles recently about the dramatic increase in discount real estate brokerages and the growing for-sale-by-owner (FSBO) trend. In a soft real estate market, brokers are no longer gatekeepers of listings but instead are looking for buyers. Sellers are open to finding ways to get their home sold. Mortgage foreclosures are rising, and homes are being sold at auction. At the same time, an increasing number of listings are on the Web, available for all to see. The federal government has brought restraint-of-trade law suits against the National Realtor Association. This is creating a perfect storm that will bring about dramatic change in the real estate brokerage business in the next two years.

A recent front-page article in the *New York Times* highlighted the fact that, in the six-year period from 1998 to 2004, people in Madison, Wisconsin, who sold their homes through agents did not get a higher price than those who sold their homes themselves.[1] When agent commissions were factored in, the for-sale-by-owner people came out ahead. This, of course, refutes one of the axioms of the brokerage business: people who use brokers get a higher price. The caveat to this story is that Madison is a city that has had a long and successful history of FSBO and that the local FSBO Web site is well used and well respected. Therefore, this data is local and cannot represent the national market. However, this is the beginning of a trend. What did not exist 10 years ago is rapidly becoming a trend. I regularly see FSBO signs in front of houses in Chicago, something I rarely saw 10 years ago.

There are now state and regional discount real estate brokerage firms expanding aggressively across the country. A recent story in the *Chicago Sun-Times* profiled what happens when this new trend butts up against the old way of doing business. A young couple chose to sign up with an online discount broker. The deal was simple: the couple would do all the legwork, the discount broker would handle the paperwork, and on closing would rebate 75 percent of the 2.5-percent commission paid to the buyer's agent. The couple spent a lot of time looking for the right house. When they found it and contacted the traditional broker who represented the seller, that broker refused to work with a discount broker. It took the buyers' attorney to firmly suggest the illegality of that stance to bring the traditional broker around. Shortly after the closing, the couple received a check for $13,000 from their discount brokerage, money that traditionally would go into the broker's pocket. A key component to this story is that it will only work for buyers or sellers who are very comfortable online, as that's where most of the interaction takes place.

A majority of real estate listings are now on the Web. Vast amounts of real estate data, including sales prices, are also on the Web. If buyers or sellers are interested in doing the work, doing the research, and spending some time on the effort, why should the broker be paid full commission? To those real estate brokers who might be angry reading these words, please let me ask you a question: if you had researched a stock and had made the decision to buy, would you pay full commission on the transaction, or would you go to a Web-based discount brokerage firm? If you do all the work and know what you want to buy, why should you pay the full-service brokerage fee? Ten years ago full-service stockbrokers were resistant to change, and look what happened to them.

This force of disintermediation is too powerful to resist. I predict the national real estate market will recover from its current recession in 2009, and, when it does, the residential real estate business will look distinctly different than it did in the heady marketplace of 2005.

CHAPTER 9:
INTELLECTUAL PROPERTY, THE
WEALTH OF THE SHIFT AGE

INTELLECTUAL PROPERTY, REPLACING physical property, is the foremost financial asset of our time. Its emergence is a logical evolution: in the Agricultural Age we valued land; in the Industrial Age we valued manufacturing and production; and in the Information Age and now on into the Shift Age we value knowledge.

"Intellectual Property Is the New Valuation" takes a historical perspective on the increasing importance of intellectual property. Then "A Historic Day for Intellectual Property," "The Financial Exchange for the 21st Century," and "The Merchant Banker of Intellectual Capital" look at some recent efforts to facilitate the exchange of intellectual property and formalize IP valuation.

Intellectual Property Is the New Valuation

April 12, 2007

In the last 10,000 years there have been three ages of humanity. The first was the Agricultural Age, which began around 8,000 BC when humanity stopped being nomadic and began to put down roots, literally. The advent of agriculture allowed humanity to build a social fabric that was placed-based and that created values around land and the process of growing food.

The Agricultural Age lasted until the late 1700s, when the Industrial Age first began in Europe. With the commercial use of the new invention called the steam engine, the world started to change rapidly, with mechanized production, transport, and the growing importance of cities as places of production and distribution. If you live in an urban area, what you see was largely created during the Industrial Age. Approximately 30 years ago the Information Age began in developed countries. This age was initiated by communications satellites, computers, and historically unprecedented numbers of college graduates. The number of white-collar workers surpassed the number of blue-collar, or production, workers for the first time.

Each of these ages created not only new economic structures, activities, and workplaces, they also created new values. The dominant value of the Agricultural Age was land and the wealth that came from the land; large landowners were the wealthy. Once the Industrial Age reached maturity, the new economic value became production, which created wealth. The wealthy initially were the early captains of industry, the robber barons, whose colossal enterprises created unprecedented riches. This wealth migrated to the stock markets, where it was defined by the amount of stock one owned. Today's legacy of the economic values of the Agricultural Age and Industrial Age are ownership of real estate and equities.

The Information Age created the new values of data, information, decentralization, innovation, and intellectual property. Fifty years ago the major exports of the United States were produced goods. Today a major category is intellectual property in the form of movies, music, books, software, video games, and higher education. It has been clear to me for years that we are now actually beyond the Information Age, or the

Knowledge Age, and in the Shift Age, where what is important economically is intellectual property (IP). A company's patents and IP are now more important and more valuable than all its machines, transport vehicles, and office equipment combined.

In recent years, I've noticed a trailing perception left over from the Industrial Age when it comes to apparent value. It's called the Dow Jones Industrial Average, even though a number of companies that are part of this group are not industrial. I intuitively knew that IP was becoming more important than production, but I wasn't sure, not being a finance person, what the financial markets were doing to reflect this incredibly significant change in the world. Last week I found out.

I attended a meeting with a colleague in the offices of Ocean Tomo. Ocean Tomo calls itself the Intellectual Capital Merchant Banc. Simply put, the company specializes in valuation, management, measurement, and transactions of intellectual property. Ocean Tomo is well known in the IP and corporate finance worlds as the company that is almost single-handedly creating all aspects of the new IP marketplace.

In the meeting with CEO James Malackowski and members of his executive team, I got detailed confirmation of what I knew intuitively must be true: that the value of IP, or intangible value, of companies is now much more important than tangible assets. Malackowski gave me a chart that was quite clear. In 1975, at the very beginning of the Information Age, 16.8 percent of the market capitalization of the S&P 500 was from intangible assets. By 1995 that number had grown to 68.4 percent, and in 2005 it was up to 79.7 percent, where I imagine it will level off in the years ahead. In the historically short time of 30 years there has been a fundamental shift in the concept of value, not unlike the transition from the land values of the Agricultural Age to the production values of the Industrial Age.

How to reflect this transition in the financial marketplace? Ocean Tomo has come up with a deeply researched and incredibly simple way: the Ocean Tomo 300 Patent Index, or OTPAT. To quote the American Stock Exchange's succinct description, "The Ocean Tomo 300 is the first major broad-based market equity index to be launched in 35 years and follows the progression from the Dow Jones Industrial Average in 1896 to the Standard & Poor's 500 in 1957 and the NASDAQ Composite Index in 1971." While those mentioned indexes will continue to be important, as a futurist, I fully believe that the Ocean Tomo 300 Patent Index could well become the most important stock index in the next 20 years. The other indexes are based on Industrial Age constructs and have adapted and revised themselves to better reflect the Information Age. The Ocean Tomo index is the only one based solely on the values of our current age.

There are always companies and individuals who step into the breach, who jump into the future and show the world a new direction. To find one doing just that in such a hugely important space and whose operating premise is so historically important and correct was nothing less than thrilling for me. Knowing something would have to come into existence and then finding it is exhilarating.

• • •

A Historic Day for Intellectual Property

April 24, 2007

My recent column "Intellectual Property Is the New Valuation" discusses the historical context for the emergence of intellectual property as the new and most important valuation of a company. While this point of view is becoming more mainstream every day, the current problem is that there is no liquid market to help determine actual valuations.

Corporations and individuals can easily monetize their real estate holdings, their heavy and office equipment, and just about any hard asset they have. As noted in the earlier column, almost 80 percent of the value of the S&P 500 companies is their intellectual property, or IP. There are all kinds of markets to monetize the remaining 20 percent of a company's assets, but what about the IP?

Last week I witnessed the beginning of the answer to this question. If you believe, as I do, that IP is becoming the dominant asset in commerce in this new century, then last week's activities in Chicago are significant. The company mentioned in the earlier column, Ocean Tomo, held two days of meetings for IP specialists from around the world. I attended two events that suggest the coming future of the IP marketplace.

The first event was a town hall meeting on two major proposals: creating an Intellectual Property Enterprise Zone and establishing an Intellectual Property Exchange. The Enterprise Zone, developed with help from the Chicago Chamber of Commerce, the City of Chicago, and the State of Illinois, would be a physical marketplace dedicated to technology licensing and IP monetization. As envisioned, the Zone would be a facility that would have offices for more than 100 corporate IP professionals from companies with substantial IP portfolios. The idea is that physical proximity, familiarity, and an ongoing effort by professionals to value IP through transactions will establish a new playing field. Given the huge value of companies' IP assets, maintaining a small office and a small staff of one or two in Chicago to help monetize IP should not be an issue. This is one of those ideas so simple yet profound that one wonders why it doesn't exist already.

The Intellectual Property Exchange would establish a new IP-based financial market. The establishment of this exchange would allow the trading of a wide range of IP-related products such as IP-related indexes, futures, and options; IP-backed bonds; and patent-rich company IPOs. This entire exchange would build off the new Ocean Tomo 300, an index of IP-rich companies that was launched late last year and is traded on the American Stock Exchange. Obviously, the Exchange is a much more complex entity to create than the Zone. The planned launch dates are summer 2008 for the Zone and early 2010 for the Exchange.

During the town hall meeting, Professor James J. Angel from the Georgetown University Graduate School of Business, an expert on the history of financial markets, made a straightforward and compelling presentation. Some highlights from his presentation are worth noting. IP in the world has an estimated value of $5.5 trillion. This number includes patents from such patent-heavy industries as pharmaceuticals, technology, energy extraction, and manufacturing, not to mention copyrights on movies, books, and Internet properties. Like real estate, IP is illiquid, and each piece is different; unlike real estate, there are few traded financial instruments that have IP as the underlying asset. While there are a great number of financial exchanges in the world, there are no IP exchanges. Angel suggested that, during the course of history, markets have been created to facilitate trade of all kinds and that such markets were created when the time was right. I concur with his conclusion that now is the historically right time to create an IP financial marketplace.

It is interesting to note that Sears, a quintessentially Industrial Age retailer, just secured a $1.8 billion bond with the IP from the Craftsman, Kenmore, and DieHard brands.

Later that same day, Ocean Tomo held its third live IP auction. With hundreds of people in attendance and motivated bidders on the phone, the auction was lively. In the first hour the world record of $1.4 million for a patent, set at the last Ocean Tomo auction, was broken, with a successful bid of $2.75 million for a patent described in the catalog as covering "various methods of communicating, managing, and storing data" for digital and home media. Fifteen minutes later there was a winning bid of $2.6 million for "matching first and second mobile communications devices." While a number of lower-priced patents did not sell, the general trend was rapid and aggressive bidding. These prices for IP, as the prices in the world of art auctions do for art, serve as benchmarks for the valuation of IP worldwide. Unlike car or art auctions, where you can see the physical merchandise, what the audience was shown on large screens were patent schematics, largely unintelligible to this viewer. It is a new world.

The creation of liquid markets for intellectual property is one of the most significant and historically timely developments in the world today. Twenty years from now the financial world will look back and acknowledge that this was the beginning of a new stage in the financial history of the world.

• • •

The Financial Exchange for the 21st Century

August 1, 2007

The New York Stock Exchange (NYSE) was founded in 1817, some 50 years after the beginning of the Industrial Age. The need for the NYSE was, in part, a result of the transition of the U.S. economy from one completely agricultural to one rapidly becoming industrial. During the 1800s the NYSE became increasingly important to the economy as a financial market that could both provide financial liquidity to listed companies and establish valuation and worth of all companies traded.

In the 20th century the NYSE was joined by other exchanges such as the American Stock Exchange (AMEX) and the National Association of Securities Dealers Automated Quotations system (NASDAQ). These exchanges served to provide liquidity, valuation, and a way that investors could own and trade shares of companies. These markets therefore became central to the miracle that was the U.S. economy of the past 100 years.

Some 30 years ago, however, the Industrial Age started to give way to the Information Age, and something interesting began to happen. The value of hard assets as a percentage of total corporate value started to decline. In 1975 16.8 percent of the market capitalization of the S&P 500 was from intangible assets. By 1995 that number had grown to 68.4 percent, and in 2005 it was up to 79.7 percent, where I imagine it will level off in the years ahead. Another way of stating this is that intellectual property, or intellectual capital, has become the dominant value in America's corporate world. The patents, trademarks, and the ideas of a company are now four times more valuable than its machinery, buildings, and other hard assets.

This presents a problem. While there are many marketplaces that corporate executives can go to for the liquidation of unneeded machinery and real estate, there is no liquid marketplace where intellectual capital can be monetized. If 80 percent of the value of a corporation cannot be readily liquidated except by the selling of the entire company, there is no way to free up unneeded assets for cash. Currently the way that companies convert their intellectual capital into cash is through a very long and subjective process. The in-house lawyer or head of IP gets on a plane and flies to meet his or her counterpart at another company where they begin a discussion about what respective patents might be worth. All this is done with poker faces and can last for months. Since there is no market measure of the IP value, third parties are brought in to evaluate and help the two companies reach a valuation of the patents.

This situation absolutely demands the creation of an IP marketplace that can help companies monetize their intellectual capital as the stock markets have allowed them to do with their stock. Three months ago I wrote the column "A Historic Day for Intellectual Property" about what may well have started the movement toward such an exchange. Two weeks ago I was fortunate to witness and participate in the next step toward this historical necessity: Ocean Tomo, the company leading the way in this endeavor, hosted the IPX Chicago Symposium to formally launch the creation of both an Intellectual Property Enterprise Zone and the Intellectual Property Exchange Chicago.

While the meetings last spring were hopeful and introductory, the recent meetings were much more organizational with a feeling that the rubber is beginning to meet the road. The attendees, in addition to Ocean Tomo CEO James Malackowski and his top executives, included Robert C. Cresanti, under secretary of commerce for technology; J. Steven Landefeld, director of the Bureau of Economic Analysis; Bob Shearer, CEO for the Center of Advanced Technologies; and the young and dynamic Chris Israel, the U.S. coordinator for international intellectual property enforcement. Also in attendance were IP executives from numerous Fortune 500 companies, several large law firms, the State of Illinois, the City of Chicago, several Chicago financial exchanges, and universities. There were even a few representatives of hedge funds. Everyone named in this paragraph was pretty clear that the historical moment for the creation of an IP exchange was now and that, if it wasn't going to be in the United States, either Europe or China might soon take global leadership on this essential new marketplace.

The first step, to be launched next year, is the Intellectual Property Enterprise Zone. It is to be an actual physical location in Chicago where representatives of corporations from around the world can set up small one- to three-person offices staffed by their IP professionals. This will allow companies to interact on a daily basis, greatly facilitating discussions about and transactions for IP assets. This is the first step to replace the arduous, time-intensive, flying-around-the-country method described above.

The second step, to be launched a year or two after the IP Enterprise Zone, is the IP Exchange (IPX), also in Chicago. This is much more complex and will take some time to perfect and develop. There will be many different investment possibilities. Companies will be certified for equity listing based on the quality of their IP portfolios. There will be IP-related indexes based on patents, brands, trademarks, and copyrights. Building on an emerging market reality, IPX will be the marketplace for IP-backed debt offerings. In addition it is expected that the IPX will be a place for patent-rich companies to make initial public offerings to investors. All in all, the IPX will become the world's first exchange for the monetization of IP and will, in many ways, mirror the functional necessity and operational efficiency of today's major stock exchanges.

The IP Enterprise Zone and the IPX ride the wave of historical inevitability. Whether you refer to the current era as the Information Age, the Knowledge Age, or the Shift Age, intellectual property is the emerging and dominant asset of our time. As the great stock markets were needed to amplify and enable the Industrial Age, so now will the IPX, and other IP exchanges that will follow, do the same for the global economy of this century. This is why I think IP valuation is one of the most exciting and significant developments in the world today. It is transformative and essential at the same time. Stay tuned.

• • •

The Merchant Banker of Intellectual Capital

October 8, 2007

Intellectual property (IP) has always been important. In the last 30 years, it has replaced hard assets as the most important part of corporate valuations. In the Shift Age, IP will be the most important asset that any individual or company can own. The ability to create value, transactions, liquidity, and ultimately an open marketplace of intellectual capital (IC) is therefore one of the most important historical developments that lie ahead for the emerging global economy.

I have written before about the efforts of one company, Ocean Tomo, to lead the way to this new future of IC. Here now is an interview with James Malackowski, founder, president, and CEO of Ocean Tomo.

Ocean Tomo is an integrated Intellectual Capital Merchant Banc® firm providing valuation, investment and risk management, and corporate finance and expert services. Ocean Tomo assists clients—corporations, law firms, governments, and institutional investors—in realizing Intellectual Capital Equity® value, broadly defined. Subsidiaries of Ocean Tomo include Ocean Tomo Auctions, LLC; Ocean Tomo Asset Management, LLC; and Ocean Tomo Capital, LLC, which publishes the Ocean Tomo 300® Patent Index (Amex: OTPAT), the Ocean Tomo 300® Patent Growth Index (Amex: OTPATG), and the Ocean Tomo 300® Patent Value Index (Amex: OTPATV).

Malackowski is an internationally recognized leader in the field of intellectual property management as well as a noted expert in business valuation and intellectual property strategy. He is a member of the IP Hall of Fame Academy and was recognized in 2007 as one of the 50 most influential people in intellectual property.

Houle: Jim, how did you first get interested in intellectual property? Was it some event or personal experience?

Malackowski: My career in IP was a classic example of being in the right place at the right time. After graduating from Notre Dame in the mid 1980s, I chose to work with a small dispute and contract accounting firm as preparation for what I thought would be a career in business law. Given my family's background as small business owners, I requested to work on smaller rather than larger matters for the firm. In practice, this meant working on the firm's first patent accounting involving the swirl flame of a blowtorch rather than a nuclear power plant. After the first patent accounting, I was staffed on the second. After the third, I was an expert. Fortunately, I could sense that IP was becoming relatively more important to each of my clients and at that point made a decision to focus my attention on this emerging asset class.

Houle: When did you decide to make intellectual property and the IP marketplace your career and life's work?

Malackowski: Three years after my first assignment valuing IP for disputes I experienced two concurrent events that set my career path. First, I was asked by a client to value IP for a transaction rather than a dispute, and my then-employer required that I reject the assignment as "impossible" and not be covered by their professional insurance. Second, the firm I was working for was sold to an international advertising agency wanting to branch into consulting. Although I had progressed rapidly to the level just below partner, I would not share in the sale proceeds. At that point, age 25, I decided I would start my own practice to focus exclusively on IP valuation, both for disputes and transactions. That turned out to be a good decision.

Houle: When was it that you truly saw that intellectual property would become the dominant asset in the Information Age? I know you call it the Knowledge Age, and I call our current times the Shift Age, but regardless of the name, in the post-Industrial Age the value of IP has surpassed the value of hard corporate assets. When did this become trend become clear to you?

Malackowski: From the mid 1980s to the late 1990s I was buried deep in the forest of IP-based client work. After we sold the business in 1999, I had a three-year remaining non-compete to extinguish. This gave me plenty of time to think. I was fortunate enough to spend this time first with the private equity firm that funded our sale and then with a boutique investment bank. This change of venue, combined with a lot of reading about the development of merchant banking as an industry 200 years prior, led to my recognizing that IP was an emerging asset class and my thoughts for developing a strategy to monetize the asset across traditional models.

Houle: When you founded Ocean Tomo, what was your vision for the company? You call Ocean Tomo "the Intellectual Capital Merchant Banc." Please explain.

Malackowski: Ocean Tomo's mission is based clearly on my interpretation of the merchant banking model developed by Morgan Grenfell in the mid 1800s. I desired to be "all things finance" related to the asset I knew best—intellectual property. The notion of combining valuation, investment, dispute accounting, risk management, and corporate finance advisory services around a single asset class under a unified name was not mine. I simply applied lessons I read to IP.

Houle: Please explain what the Ocean Tomo 300 indexes are, how they are compiled, and where and how they are traded.

Malackowski: There are countless articles that describe the construction and purpose of the Ocean Tomo family of indexes. Briefly, we wanted to create a broad market measure of innovation by allowing investors to buy a collection of stocks with strong patents. It is very similar to the S&P 500, though, rather than the 500 largest companies, it is the 300 companies with the best patents for their size and investment style (i.e., relative value). The Ocean Tomo 300® Patent Index and its growth and value derivative are all priced on the American Stock Exchange with exchange-traded funds offered by Claymore Securities (e.g., AMEX: OTP). As of this writing, year-to-date performance has been more than 700 bps [basis points] above the S&P. Starting later this year, we will be offering a new index, the IPX Composite, which will include not only the Ocean Tomo 300 firms but others with qualified patent portfolios. Further detail can be found at http://www.oceantomoindexes.com.

Houle: It strikes me that the Ocean Tomo 300 Patent Index is the only equities index that truly and purely values corporate intellectual capital. Since IC is the valuation in ascendancy, it would make sense that the Ocean Tomo 300 should and will become one of if not the most influential stock indexes of this new century. Do you agree, and, if so, when do you think that might happen?

Malackowski: Clearly, we agree. In fact, the American Stock Exchange has already proclaimed the Ocean Tomo 300® Patent Index to be the first new major market index in 35 years following the DOW, S&P,

and NASDAQ. In less than one year since inception, the index is routinely cited alongside the DOW and NASDAQ on daily market reports. It is included in the most respected news media listings of major indexes, and it became investible through ETFs [exchange-traded funds] almost immediately upon inception. I think we are well on our way of achieving the goal of educating the market about the indexes, which we believe will result in the influential position your question suggests.

Houle: Please explain to my readers the current state of the IP marketplace: how does IP get valued, and how do transactions get done?

Malackowski: The IP market is clearly emerging. Most transactions are still valued and executed in a private, one-off, highly inefficient way. Our ratings software, public auctions, and pending IP trade exchange are changing the way business is done. IP is spreading from a topic of the general counsel to a focus of the CFO. In our view, this remains a long-term transition but the next five years will see tremendous progress. As an example, less than 18 months ago, the idea of a routine large-scale public auction for IP was viewed as silly. Today it is already an accepted part of the IP solution set.

Houle: The IP auctions that Ocean Tomo initiated in 2006 seem to be a step to create a more liquid and transparent IP marketplace. I gather the auctions have really been a success given the large sums being paid. I know the spring 2007 one I attended in Chicago broke some records. How are they going, and what do you think the future of IP auctions will look like?

Malackowski: Prior to the first press release announcing a live multi-lot auction of IP, we made a three-year commitment to the process of building an auction marketplace. This commitment was also made public to both instill confidence in new market participants as much as to lock ourselves into a position that could not be easily altered. To date, each auction has exceeded our plans and expectations. We believe that the live auctioning of IP will be a permanent marketplace. That said, we have also proclaimed our desire from the beginning to obsolete the auction floor for most transactions by creating a traded exchange for IP (see http://www.ipxchicago.com). This transition will begin in 2010 and should be fully complete within three years.

Houle: As you know, I have written about the steps you are taking to change this. Please explain what they are and the timeline for bringing them online. What is the IP Exchange?

Malackowski: IPX Chicago is a traded exchange for intellectual property that seeks to bring the efficiency of existing equity and commodity indexes to IP as an asset class. We expect to launch IPX as a separate exchange on January 1, 2010, with four products: equity listings, IP-based indexes and related futures and options, Tradable Technology Baskets™, and Unit License Rights™. Ocean Tomo, as founder of IPX, is working today to immediately post industry-based indexes of patent value (e.g., the notional value of all patents comprising hybrid electric vehicles) in major financial publications and complete a number of beta trades within the next six months.

Houle: What has been the reaction of corporations both in the United States and around the world to these initiatives? Are any taking the first steps toward full participation? Anything you can share?

Malackowski: As a career entrepreneur, the toughest part of my day is understanding the prevailing—and no doubt prudent—attitudes of large corporations. As we have introduced each initiative, the results have been similar: an early and broad recognition that the IP market needs such a solution, a grave resistance to be the first to participate, and gradual adoption and participation. Given that, we are happy with the actual results thus far; we are very excited about what we see as the growth for these new markets as more and more firms adopt.

Houle: Jim, as a futurist, I look at the waves of history to better see what lies ahead. You will recall that when we first met I was thrilled because I believed that the transition from the Industrial Age to the Information/Knowledge Age and on to the Shift Age dictated the need for a change in the evaluation of wealth and assets, but I had yet to meet people who were doing the heavy lifting to manifest this change. It seems to me that you, your company, and its vision are part of something historically inevitable and timely. Do you see it that way? Please, no false modesty.

Malackowski: We clearly see ourselves as a part—a catalyst—of an extraordinary transition. The movement to an intangible-based economy is every bit as significant as was the Industrial Revolution a century ago.

Houle: It could be said therefore that Ocean Tomo—and perhaps other companies like it—is representative of an idea whose time has come. That is the most powerful force there is. Do you agree?

Malackowski: We hope a rising tide will raise all boats and are happy to be on our own little ship out at sea.

Houle: Thank you so much for taking the time for this interview.

CHAPTER 10:
THE MORPHING OF MEDIA

MEDIA, LIKE EVERYTHING in the Shift Age, is changing rapidly. Broadband Internet has arrived and recently passed the threshold of being in 50 percent of American homes. Its effects are felt as all forms of media reassess the value of their content, the distribution of that content, the underlying business model, and how to survive and thrive in a dramatically changed world.

With a historical perspective on media's evolution, "Broadband... Finally!" looks at the pivotal influence of widespread high-speed Internet access on society. In the post-digital landscape described in "High-touch Media," engagement with customers, not ratings or statistics, is the true measure of the success—and the viability—of media. "A Media Milestone" and "Three Deaths of a Media Icon" portray two different responses to the Internet's encroachment on traditional print media. And "A Book Convention: In the Year 2025" posits the book publishing business, in this digital age, is ripe for transformation.

Broadband...Finally!

June 6, 2006

The rapid growth of broadband, high-speed Internet hookups during the last year is impressive and speaks to the widening demographic and economic base of broadband users.

According to a survey from the Pew Internet & American Life Project, broadband adoption increased 59 percent among households with incomes between $30,000 and $50,000 from March 2005 to March 2006.[1] It increased 40 percent in households earning less than $30,000 and increased 121 percent in black households. This is incredible growth in economic and demographic segments that had heretofore lagged far behind more upscale homes and white households. One of the reasons for this is the drop in pricing for both DSL and cable. Middle- and lower-income households still lag behind more affluent ones with the $30,000 to $50,000 households at 43 percent compared to 68-percent penetration in households with more than $75,000 in annual income. Overall, 42 percent of adult Americans have broadband at home, compared to 30 percent a year ago. This means we can expect penetration to exceed 50 percent in the next year.

To put these numbers in perspective, the only comparable periods of new media growth on a percentage basis were the early 1950s with TV and the late 1990s with dial-up Internet. When you factor in the fact that there are almost twice as many households in the United States today as there were in 1950, the growth in actual number of households is certainly one of the greatest single-year growth records for a new medium in U.S. history. When you compare the 42 percent total of broadband households with the 4 percent in 2000, it becomes clear we are in the midst of explosive growth. And this is on top of the estimated 70 percent of U.S. employees who have access to broadband at work. We have entered the age of broadband...finally.

Why do I say "finally"? Well, for me, the experience of reading these numbers was almost one of déjà vu and not surprising in the least. As far back as 1998 I was giving speeches saying that the power of the Internet would not begin to be realized until broadband reached critical mass at 40- to 60-percent penetration. I said this at a time when people were marveling at the revolutionary power of the Internet, even when the general experience of it was with slow dial-up. When asked when the United States, which lagged behind a number of other countries in broadband penetration, might reach this critical mass, my best guess was "sometime during the first decade of the new millennium." When one expects something to happen for such a long time, when it actually does happen, it is no big deal. It is almost as though the expectation was the experience, and the actual reality just confirmation.

Why was I so certain the Internet would not realize its full potential until the majority of the population could experience it in high speed? As a student of media history, I know that each new medium that comes along expands on all prior media, in terms of function and effect. The first mass medium was the book, which came about because of Gutenberg's invention of the moveable-type printing press. Manuscripts that had been read by hundreds of people were now books read by tens of thousands of people. This led to the next print medium, the newspaper, which allowed people to read about events they hadn't experienced and created a larger sense of community than could be created by word of mouth. The newspaper was followed by the magazine, which brought pictures and color to the arena of print media. Then along came radio, which was the first non-print medium; it brought sound to the equation and thus allowed information and entertainment to move quickly and immediately through the air. Live radio programs created communities that were no longer geographically limited. Then television followed, adding sight and motion to radio's sound and expanding electronic media exponentially. It could be argued that television was the single most influential cultural force of the second half of the 20th century. It was the beginning of the global village as described by Marshall McLuhan. The last 20 years of the century saw the explosive growth of cable television, which brought the concept of targeted audience programming to television yet continued to add to the mass of the medium. So each new medium added to and expanded on all prior media.

When the Internet became a mass medium in the 1990s, the revolutionary potential was obvious. What bothered me, however, was that, in appearance and in delivery of content, it was more like newspapers and magazines, without any of the innovations of radio, television, and cable television. Everything on the Internet at that time looked like newspapers and magazines; everything was text; everything was columns, squares, and oblongs, static on the page. This broke the historical precedent of each medium building on and expanding all prior media. It was puzzling. Then when I was introduced to the concept of bandwidth and speed of data transmission I experienced the aha moment: when the pipes broaden, then video can be viewed in real time! When it is in a fully broadband environment, that is when the Internet can begin to fully reach its potential. So, to adapt Samuel Beckett, I've been waiting for broadband.

Why is broadband so exciting? It is the first new medium in the history of humanity that can fully replicate and fully deliver the promise of all prior media. One can read newspapers and magazines online. One can listen to radio online. One can watch television and cable television programs online. That alone is exciting: all prior media is contained in broadband Internet. What is really exciting, revolutionary, and transformative, however, is the fact that it is the first medium without content and distribution gatekeepers. Everyone can post words, music, discussions, pictures, and video online for the entire world to consume. The Internet has become the first one-to-many, many-to-one, and one-to-one medium in the history of humanity. Now that is something that makes a futurist weak in the knees when thinking about the Internet's potential in and for the future.

This explosion in the use of broadband is often referred to as Internet 2.0, using the computer software model of numerically sequencing upgrades. Internet 1.0 was the explosive growth during the dial-up years of the mid to late 1990s. That's fine, but the question is, what is the definition of Internet 3.0 or Internet 2.5? I certainly can attempt to create definitions and will do so in the future. The two things I want to cover today are the word *broadband* and my experience reading the Pew Internet & American Life Project report.

The current terminology is "high-speed Internet hookups." OK, that's fine. It is descriptive but also temporary and transactional. "High-speed" is relative to "dial-up." What happens when speed increases? Then we move to "super high-speed"? If, compared to trains, propeller airplanes were high-speed, what were jet airplanes? The second part of the phrase is transactional, as either a phone company via DSL or a cable company with a cable modem made the connection and got a subscriber. Cable subscriptions do not describe cable TV but the connection to it. Basically, "high-speed Internet hookups" is simply a temporary term used to measure growth in transactions.

Why do I care? I continue to use the word "broadband" to describe this growing media, and people say, "You mean high-speed Internet access?" Aaah, we are such lemmings when it comes to high-tech terminology, striving to sound cool, hip, and current. I have low tolerance for overuse of trendy terminology.

• • •

High-touch Media

September 15, 2006

Three months ago, I had an aha experience that led me to the realization that we are in an era of high-touch media.[2]

I was on a Newark-bound plane out of Chicago that had a scheduled departure time of 4:30 p.m. Due to "weather" and "flow control," the departure time came and went. We rolled out on the tarmac and waited in a long line of planes. 5:30 came and went, then 6:30. So here we all were on a completely full airplane at dinnertime, with no food on board, and people getting surly. All of a sudden the flight attendant came on the intercom to announce that, due to the generosity of two passengers, everyone would be getting a free Dove candy bar. Two employees of Dove were going to a candy convention with their new product line, so they had a duffle bag of candy bars.

Needless to say, the mood on the plane elevated dramatically as empty stomachs were filled and everyone was on a mild chocolate sugar high. The entire plane was talking about Dove candy bars, and there was a line of passengers thanking the two Dove employees. This was a high-touch experience for the entire plane. For me it was the beginning of a new way to look at advertising.

In this post-digital media landscape, where what used to work no longer feels adequate and what we think might work is yet to be tested, we have moved into a completely new time: the time of high-touch media.

First, let's break the phrase down to its component parts, according to *Merriam-Webster's Online Dictionary* (http://www.m-w.com).

- *High* is defined as "upward," "elevated," "active," "most fully developed," "exalted," "rich," "intoxicated," "stupefied," and "luxurious."
- *Touch* is defined as "to bring a bodily part into contact with," "to perceive through the tactile sense," "to strike or push lightly," "to lay hands upon," to "become involved with," "to get to," "reach," "to

leave a mark or impression on," "to move to sympathetic feeling," "to make a brief or incidental stop," and "to cause to be briefly in contact or conjunction with something."

- The definition of *media* includes this on usage: "The singular *media* and its plural *medias* seem to have originated in the field of advertising over 70 years ago; they are apparently still so used without stigma in that specialized field. In most other applications, *media* is used as a plural of *medium*. The great popularity of the word in references to the agencies of mass communication is leading to the formation of a mass noun."

So what these definitions tell me is that the words *high* and *touch* are the dominant words, as the word *media* is the most narrowly defined. Since *media* is an advertising word used by advertising and communication people, people in those industries need to be educated on the more expansive words of *high* and *touch*. (I am not talking about upfront parties, leisure-time activities, or aspects of encounters better kept secret.)

Another way to put it is that to best understand the phrase and the concept of high-touch media, those in the advertising and communication businesses must untether themselves from standard usage of the word *media*. Think of media as a descriptor of how to message. Think of Marshall McLuhan's most famous phrase: the medium is the message. Since media and advertising are ubiquitous these days, it is all about the message—and delivering that message in such a high-touch manner that it delivers a rich, forceful impression that moves the recipient to a sympathetic feeling.

As a futurist, I look for trends, for ultra-trends, and to the directions that we as Americans and global citizens are moving. As a former media executive, I wonder what the media business and its advertising engine will look like in the coming years and decades.

I am convinced that the overarching conceptual direction is high-touch media. How do we touch our desired customer at the highest level possible? Touch them physically, emotionally, intellectually, psychologically, on their own terms, plugging into their own unique wiring. It is no longer about GRPs, reach, and frequency or other standard forms of media measurement. It is about impressions (see above definitions); and it is about engagement, but those are just part of the larger activity of high-touch media.

There is much more to write about and to explore in this new era, but let me leave you with some statements that may in fact become axioms in the very near future.

- High-touch media will be the way that companies connect with customers and potential customers from now on.
- High-touch media is the way to connect to individuals in a time of transformation and disintermediation.
- High-touch media is about you and them, one by one by one.
- High-touch media can be very physical, very emotional, and very psychological.
- High-touch media can and will be very situational.
- High-touch media incorporates every single media that has ever existed, some more than others. The situation, the product, and the target individual equal choice of media.

And the last one for today:

- High-touch media is high-cost in the short term and comparatively low-cost in the long term. Decide if you want a long-term relationship. If you do, then practice high-touch media. If your time horizon is short-term, forget about high-touch.

• • •

A Media Milestone

February 7, 2007

In my predictions for 2007, I made a specific prediction that the current Internet 2.0 boom would continue and that eyeballs, dollars, and influence would migrate from old media to the Internet. Now this isn't crystal-ball stuff. Media and advertising professionals live this reality every day. Just look at your own life. How much more time do you spend online than you did ten, five, or even two years ago? The debate is around how fast and how much, not if or when.

I read a news item in the *New York Times* the other day that was, for me, a historically and hugely symbolic underscoring of this flow of power to the Internet.[3] The world's oldest newspaper announced that it was ceasing publication on paper and would only be available online.

The Swedish newspaper PoIT—which stands for *Post- och Inrikes Tidningar*—is the world's oldest newspaper still in publication. It has been continuously published since 1645. 1645! That is just 90 years after Gutenberg printed his first Bible. The paper was founded by Queen Christina and her chancellor during the Thirty Years' War.

The editor, and only employee of PoIT, Roland Haegglund, was quoted: "The change in format is, of course, a major departure for some, possibly a little sad, but is also a natural step." Evidently PoIT had long ago ceased to be a real newspaper and had become an announcement vehicle for financial, legal, and corporate institutions. When it published its final print version on December 29, it had less than 2,000 subscribers. All that being true, it is still a hugely symbolic occurrence that the oldest newspaper on earth describes going to online as "a natural step."

The world will go on, major newspapers will continue to both publish and decline in readership, and the Internet will continue to experience explosive growth. No one outside Sweden will be materially affected by this event. Yet, however inconsequential PoIT's decision may be, in the overarching timeline of media, it is a true signpost event. A door closed, and another one swings wide open.

. . .

Three Deaths of a Media Icon

April 1, 2007

Last week it was announced that *Life* magazine would cease publication, again. This is the third death of the magazine since it was founded in 1936. *Life* was a weekly from 1936 to 1972, when it first stopped publication. It was revived as a monthly in 1978 but then shut down again in 2000. It was resurrected as a newspaper insert in 2004 but never really took hold in that iteration, which was an incredibly misguided strategy to begin with.

Life was, simply put, the greatest showcase of high-quality and historically important photographs in the middle part of the 20th century in America. Many of the greatest photographers in the country, such as Alfred Eisenstaedt and Margaret Bourke-White, dreamed of being a *Life* photographer and, in fact, became great, in part, because their photographs appeared in the magazine. I remember as a young boy the thrill of coming home from school on the day that *Life* magazine was delivered by the mailman. It was a thrill to sit down and spend an hour looking at every photograph and reading every caption. At a time when there were only five TV stations coming into homes and newscasts were 15 minutes with no video, *Life* magazine was truly a window to the world.

Why write about this when I specialize in "A Future Look at Today"? Well, the story of *Life* magazine is a story about the last 75 years of media and also a story about the failure of media executives to look to the future rather than hold on to a view of media no longer valid.

When *Life* magazine came out in 1936, radio and newspapers were the dominant mass media. *Life* was created to be the first mass visual media product in the United States. It was the main place, other than the newsreels in theaters, where America got its visual images. It visually documented the Great Depression and World War II in such a powerful way that *Life* photos are still our visual references to those two great events. It was one of the two great media properties in the empire of Henry Luce. It was sarcastically stated that "*Life* is for people who can't read, and *Time* is for people who can't think."

Life achieved a circulation in excess of seven million during the 1950s and led the dominance of the large weekly picture magazines that included *Look* and *The Saturday Evening Post*. Together, more than 20 million people read, or looked at, these three magazines every week, a number unmatched since in U.S. magazine publishing. Then something happened: broadcast network television. Between 1948 and 1955 this new medium literally exploded onto the landscape of America and, slightly later, the world. Broadcast network television became, in historically record time, the most culturally influential medium in the country. Newspapers were still the dominant news source, but, in terms of entertainment and the transmission of visual images, television won the day. It had sight, sound, and motion. How could *Life* magazine, which just had one of those three, compete? It couldn't.

The circulation of *Life* declined steadily from the late 1950s through the 1960s. Elvis and the Beatles were better on TV. The 1960 debates changed the political process. The Kennedy assassination weekend created the electronic global village. Vietnam was the first war brought into the living room. Why wait for the weekly pictures in *Life* when there were moving pictures with sound available every day on network television? People didn't, so *Life* shut down in 1972.

Time-Life brought the magazine back as a monthly in 1978, but somehow it was never relevant again. It was no longer the visual story of the world; it was just another magazine. More than anything else it felt like a piece of nostalgia. Its time had passed. Television had destroyed the picture magazine, as later the 24-hour news channels made *Time* magazine and the other news weeklies less relevant. Why wait a week for news or news analysis when it was availably every day, every hour?

The historical insularity of media executives is highlighted by the way Time Warner re-launched the iconic magazine in 2004. Time Warner tied it to the oldest, most rapidly declining medium: newspapers. These were print executives who saw magazines only as print products. The better choice would have been to become the photographic standard on the Internet, particularly in 2004, when it was clear that the next explosive medium would be broadband. What an opportunity lost! Think about the daily pictures you see on your home page, whether it is Yahoo or some other source. If *Life* had staked claim to the daily picture, the week's best pictures, the *Life* Web site for great photographs, it could have been slightly ahead of the curve and easily become a profitable, new iteration of an American icon. These same executives who jumped on the dying medium of newspapers are finally going online as a free resource for pictures, joining an already crowded field and without any brand clout to anyone under the age of 50. A sad ending to a glorious media vehicle.

Television and executives with blinders killed *Life* magazine. As the Internet seriously threatens newspaper and television, let us hope that the executives in these two industries look toward the future and understand that the media world is now a place of multi-platforms and that having a future look at today is essential for survival, let alone success.

• • •

A Book Convention: In the Year 2025

June 6, 2007

What is the future of the book and the book publishing industry? That question was on my mind while attending the BookExpo America convention this past weekend. In a business that is mature, leveling out or falling in unit sales, and dearly holding on to past business practices, what might be the road map for success over the next 20 years?

First, let's take a look at other content businesses, what has happened to them in this digital age, and what that might indicate for the book business.

Music is relevant in that the music business was disintermediated by the Internet. It is not relevant in that the listener still uses speakers, earphones, or ear plugs and, except for convenience and portability, doesn't really care whether the music comes from vinyl, tape, CD, or audio file (except for dedicated audiophiles). The physical listening experience is the same. Reading a book is a physical experience that would be fundamentally changed by moving to a screen.

Television and video have also been changed by the Internet. Viewing is now on a variety of screens and is becoming on-demand. Even though the variety of screens has increased, viewing is still on a screen, as it has always been. Where video can give a glimpse into the future of books is that, at least on the Internet, the power of gatekeepers has lessened. Viewer-generated content might be analogous to self-publishing via on-demand technology.

Newspapers are suffering declines in readership and revenue due to the Internet. The Internet can serve up timely news and is a much more efficient medium for classified ads. Dedicated newspaper readers enjoy the physical action of reading a newspaper, yet often accept reading the newspaper online when more convenient or when they are in a place where the physical newspaper cannot be obtained. This may be an indication of what will happen to the reading of books.

The heyday of magazines seems to have passed in terms of growth curves and cultural influence. Most have moved online, and their readerships come from both the physical and online realms. Blogs and their immediacy have affected editorial direction of magazines.

All these media are different and distinct, yet they have all been reorganized by the Internet. Music and video have also been profoundly affected by innovations in digital technology. One of the results is that the music industry has seen a steep decline in the sale of physical product as it has moved online. That development has profoundly affected the retail aspect of the business.

So what will the future of the book publishing business look like in the next few years and in 2025?

- Online sales will continue to increase as a percentage of overall sales and will represent most of the growth in the business for the next five years.
- The next sales growth spurt will occur when online retailers and then publishers sell digital downloads.
- The book business will continue to be a prime example of the long tail and will aid the growth of online retailers.
- The long-tail structure of the market will lead to niches that are organized around communities and subject categories. If one is interested in a subject, there will be specific publishers that will have developed cachet in a specific category. Publishers will become more vertical and less horizontal.
- This long-tail aspect will ultimately drive retailers to install on-site, on-demand technology, providing expanded choice and speed of sale for the customer.
- The sad downtrend of small independent bookstores closing might be reversed by this on-site, on-demand technology. This won't

happen until the cost comes down and the physical size shrinks. This has happened in every other physical technology: copiers, computers, calculators, and printers. One of the reasons that people shop at independent bookstores is the personal service and relationship with the bookseller. With less physical inventory available—one of the reasons these bookstores close—the "recommending relationship" increases in value. On-demand technology will allow retailers to sell at volumes much greater than physical inventory. Bookstores could become small, comfortable, and intimate again; have a cup of coffee while we print your book. Customers might again rely on the bookseller for guidance. This will be a unique combination of high touch and high tech.

- There will be explosive growth of author-direct-to-consumer books, fueled by on-demand printing and online retailing. Publishers will only change their business practices when brand-name authors participate in this trend.

- E-books will ultimately gain significant market share. This will occur when there is an "iPod moment": when a device comes out that is low-priced, wonderful to use, and perceived to be cool. (Steve Jobs, are you listening?) Once this occurs, there will be a rapid increase in the percentage of books sold digitally, probably leveling off around 40 to 50 percent by 2025. Impulsive buys, such as at airport bookstores, will become "purchase, plug-in, and download." While those of us who have grown up with the wonderful tactile experience of curling up with a good book may resist e-books, the younger generations who have been in front of computer screens since early childhood will intuitively embrace e-books. "What's on your e-reader?" will replace "what's on your iPod?" Already, college students are embracing online text books. Look to the youth for direction.

- Storage technology is predicted to continue to shrink in physical size and drop in cost so much that by 2025 all the new titles published in a year—in fact, the great majority of all books ever published—can be contained on a pocket-sized electronic device. Talk about publishers selling with volume discounts directly to the consumer!

- Projecting green consciousness, the book publishing industry will move to digital publishing. Consumers who still buy physical books will become more selective. When environmentalists focus on the publishing industry, digital publishing and distribution and e-books will be the "correct" position.

- All this emphasis on digital will mean that physical books will be greater in value and less disposable. People will read most books in digital form but will allow themselves to have, say, the complete works of Hemingway in physical form.

So, in conclusion, the book publishing business is about to undergo a transformation that is historically unique. For the first time in history the physicality of the book as a mass-market product will end for a large percentage of readers. Retailing will change dramatically. Publishers will become more category-specific. Publishers and authors will sell direct to consumers once the digital book takes off.

Fortunately, regardless of what form and how and from whom the book is purchased, there will always be the experience of a good read, which is the experiential, irreplaceable product of the book publishing industry.

CHAPTER 11:
CULTURE AT THE BEGINNING
OF THE SHIFT AGE

T HE PARADOXICAL PERMANENCE of change in the Shift Age has had
profound effects on our individual daily lives and our culture as a
whole. With so much change collapsed into such a short time, it can be
hard to fully understand the subtle and not-so-subtle adaptations that
surround us.

This chapter is a reflection—sometimes appreciative and sometimes
critical—on recent cultural and societal changes: the rise of coffee consumption; the scarcity of water; the decline in smoking; the assimilation
of new phenomena, from movies to rock and roll to video games; even an
expanding definition of life.

In the Future, Let's All Get Caught Napping

April 3, 2006

Recently there have been a number of articles in the mainstream
media about sleep. They all take the general point of view that Amer-

icans are sleep-deprived, that we need eight hours of sleep but aren't getting it, and that this sleep deprivation takes its toll across all aspects of society.

Many of these articles have suggested reasons for this growing sleep deprivation. They mention that in this age of ever-increasing connectedness we always have another call to make, another e-mail to write, another Web site to visit; we are obsessed with our connectedness. They usually profile some poor soul with numbed thumbs who is addicted to his Blackberry or some road warrior who crosses time zones so often she falls asleep at strange times.

The prevailing wisdom about sleep is that we all need eight hours a day. We heard this from our mothers. We read about getting a good eight hours of sleep and spending a third of our time sleeping. It is a rare night that I get eight hours of sleep. When I ask people how much sleep they get a night, I rarely hear "eight hours." More often than not, I get the answer "six hours, maybe six and a half," or "I only need four or five hours' sleep," usually said with chest-thumping braggadocio. Few of us are getting what we are supposed to get in terms of sleep at night. No wonder Starbucks is thriving and Red Bull has spawned dozens of imitators.

Various new businesses have jumped into the economic space of sleep deprivation. Big pharmas sell hundreds of millions of sleeping pills. There are noise reduction ear phones, blindfolds, and white-noise machines. There's a company that rents out nap pods for 20-minute intervals to bleary-eyed New Yorkers. Nap pods—now that got me thinking about sleep through the ages.

In the Agricultural Age, economic activity was centered on the farm, which was worked during the day to produce the crops. In the Industrial Age, economic activity was centered on the factory, where goods were produced during the day (at least until artificial illumination allowed for double shifts). Work during the day; sleep during the night.

Today we are just 200 years removed from an America that was largely agricultural. Most people lived on or near farms, and the rhythm of life was tied to the rhythm of nature. Time was measured by seasons and by days. Spring was the planting season, summer was the growing season, and fall was the harvest season. Farmers got up at dawn, worked during the day, and then went to bed after dark. At night there were candles. With everything focused on daytime work, people slept more hours at night. That was the source of the "workday." There wasn't work to do at night. There also was a limited amount of recreation that one could do by candlelight.

Cultures located closer to the equator didn't work in the middle of the day, as it was too hot. That is when people stayed out of the sun and took naps. They shaped their sleep habits around nature, but with a different structure.

So, today in 2006, America and its economic institutions still function largely on social and time structures set up during the Agricultural Age: work during daylight; sleep when it is dark outside. We have off-shored much of our Industrial Age production and are working in the "always on" environment of the Shift Age. We work longer hours than at any time in the last century...because we can. Up at 5 a.m. to do e-mail until the kids get up, send e-mails and make phone calls while in some form of transport during the day, do Internet research after dinner, and have conference calls at 11 p.m. with India or China. No wonder we doze off in meetings, fall asleep during the commute, or lose our temper with our co-workers and kids.

It is time to update our sleep habits from the Agricultural Age to the Shift Age. We must embrace naps! Napping is a good thing. It is good for productivity, for safety, for polite social interaction, and, most importantly, for health and happiness. We need to create a culture and a workplace that support short naps. We need to create a social environment where it is a smart thing to take a nap. We need to redefine values so that napping is part of the profile of high-output, highly productive individuals, not lazy ones.

During the next 20 years, out of necessity, naps will become a much more accepted, integral, and beneficial activity. So, in the future, let's all get caught napping!

• • •

Coffee and Caffeine

November 22, 2006

We seem to have become much more of a coffee culture than ever before. It is now hard to be in any large city in the United States where there is not an abundance of places to buy coffee. Twenty years ago you could buy coffee in any neighborhood, but it was at a restaurant or a fast-food outlet. Now there are places that basically sell just coffee, with a small selection of companion snacks and cold drinks added to the mix.

Starbucks has gone from being a curiosity to one of the best-known brands in the country and, now, the world. People who 10 years ago knew coffee to be regular or decaf today speak of lattes, mochas, macchiatos, and double espressos. There are heated conversations about the comparative merits of coffee from Guatemala and Costa Rica. People in offices take turns making the mid-afternoon "Starbucks run." "Let's meet for coffee" is as common a phrase today as "let's meet for a drink" has been for decades.

There have always been cultural and culinary cycles in society. We seem to still be on the upward slope of the coffee cycle in the United States. Why? I think there are several reasons, both due to the product itself and then to all the trappings and social practices that have grown up around the product.

Simply put, caffeine is a stimulant. We all know this. One of the primary reasons we drink it is because it stimulates the nervous system and the heart. When the caffeine hits, it feels good; we feel better, more alert, perhaps even happier. Coffee is the universal pick-me-up beverage. We drink it when we haven't had enough sleep, when we have to focus on a project or paper that we don't really want to do, when we have crossed so many time zones our body rebels.

In my column "In the Future, Let's All Get Caught Napping," I suggested we're getting more and more sleep-deprived because of the "always on" culture we now live in. Everything is available 24 hours a day. Stores are open 24 hours a day so we can always go shopping. If this is not the case in your neighborhood, the Internet is always on for those who want to shop. We can watch TV, listen to radio, surf the Internet all the time. Blockbuster movies open in theaters at midnight on Thursdays. There is always something going on in today's society. When the bars close, the breakfast places open up. So practically any form of entertainment or guilty pleasure is available to us whenever we want it. New York City used to be called "the city that never sleeps." Well, now the United States is the country that never sleeps.

Our world of work has equally expanded. We do e-mail before the kids get up; we do e-mail after the kids go to sleep. We nervously check our Blackberry or Treo while standing in line or riding in a cab. The workday is no longer 8 hours, but literally 24. Sleep at your own risk; you might fall behind! Take the afternoon off? At your own risk!

Less than 200 years ago, the United States was still an agricultural society. This meant that time was measured in seasons: the planting season of spring, the growing season of summer, the fall harvest, the hibernation of winter. A workday was defined by daylight. Remember, it was a 100 years ago that electrical lights first started to be used widely, so, even if one wanted to work after dark, it was difficult to do so. Even 50 years ago, when the Industrial Age was at its apex in the United States, the workweek was Monday to Friday and generally 9 to 5 unless one worked overtime. Now in the Shift Age, we are all working overtime, all the time. While this incredible amount of change has occurred and the speed of change has accelerated, the biology or physiology of humanity has not changed nearly as much.

Now that tobacco use has dramatically declined and most other drugs that stimulate the nervous system are illegal, what's left to keep us going? That's right: caffeine! The next time you walk into a Starbucks, particularly in the morning, look at the people waiting in line for their stimulant drink. They seem to be half-asleep, not much affect on their faces, suffering from staying up too late doing e-mail or surfing the Net or tired from poor sleep because they couldn't stop their minds from thinking about work all night.

I truly believe that the growth in coffee stores has a direct correlation to our speeded-up, evermore connected lifestyle. Cell phones, the Internet, laptops, wireless, and Starbucks all exploded on the national landscape during the same 15-year period. Looking ahead, it is clear that our coffee culture will continue to grow.

. . .

The New Coffee Culture and Why It Reflects Our Changing World

November 27, 2006

In "Coffee and Caffeine," I looked at why coffee and caffeine have become the "drugs" of the current decade. In our "always on" culture, the need for a stimulating pick-me-up is clear. I would now like to explore the other aspects of this new coffee culture, as it is the manifestation of a number of social trends and cultural dynamics that are fundamentally changing our society.

Starbucks—the biggest brand in the new wave of coffee houses—is often thought to be brilliant because it persuaded tens of millions of people to spend $4 for what had been a $1 product. I have always thought that the other brilliant thing Starbucks did was to create unlimited choice in a category that hardly had any choice. What this means is that everyone, no matter how conformist or bland in daily life can, for a couple of minutes, live in their own uniqueness. "I'll have a double decaf soy cappuccino." Or "I'll have a venti skim vanilla latte, no foam." In that moment, that individual has carved out her identity. Does she really need a double decaf soy cappuccino? Of course not. But practically unlimited choice has allowed individuals to identify themselves by the small choices they make every day. Self-definition in small ways allows us to think we are living large in the landscape of free will.

In the last 30 years we have gone from a culture of alienation to one of ultimate choice. There is no area of our lives where we do not have an unbelievably greater choice than we did 10, 20, or 30 years ago. Think about any area of popular culture: music, television channels, ways to watch video, books, video games, restaurants. Think about the super drugstores or supermarkets. How many types of salsa or vinaigrettes or cold medicines are there now versus 1980? I asked my researcher, a math graduate student, to compute the number of possible choices available to the customer at the average Starbucks. The most referenced number is around 21,000, based on popular choices. His research, factoring in all the different types of milk, sizes, kinds of drinks, flavors, and specials, yielded 189,520 permutations. Backing down to the more classic drinks and standard drink extras, he came up with a number closer to 35,000. Now compare that to walking into a coffee shop or even a coffee house 20 years ago. Starbucks then is one of the most prominent cultural examples of providing people with an opportunity to create their identity by providing practically unlimited choice.

In the last 25 years, a lot of social and cultural institutions have been dismantled, disintermediated, or just faded away as we moved from an Industrial Age society to an Information Age society. The lifelong relationship of company and employee that the post–World War II generation experienced is no longer. Much has already been written about the United States becoming a nation of free agents. Technology has allowed us to work from home or anywhere. For a lot of us, the social hub of the office is no longer. Private dining clubs have declined in numbers as the number and variety of restaurants have increased. The traditional nuclear family and all the social institutions flowing from it are no longer the norm. The speeded-up Information Age and the "always on" culture it spawned have no room for the leisurely three-martini lunch, let alone the single-glass-of-wine lunch. All of this has, to some degree, been addressed by the explosion of Starbucks and Starbucks-like coffee houses.

When we need to get out of the house because we have been working there all day, we go to Starbucks and continue to work there. When we want to meet someone for a business meeting and we don't want her to come to our home, we choose to meet at Starbucks. When we need a little bit of a sense of community, we go to our local coffee house, where the baristas know us and start preparing our "venti skim latte, no foam" as soon as they see us. When we want to have a tentative social meeting, such as meeting someone we have met on an online dating site, we meet at the coffee house. When the speed of change gets to us or something major changes in our lives or we need to take a step out of the "always on" rat race for a pause or a temporary escape, we go to Starbucks. When we feel isolated or depressed or suffer from cabin fever, we go to the 21st-century version of what Hemingway called a clean, well-lit place— Starbucks, where all is known, familiar, safe, and tasty, and the product stimulates our hearts and minds.

So the modern-day coffee house, most popularized by Starbucks, is really both a manifestation of many of the changes that have occurred in our society and an amplification of them. During the next decade Starbucks and other coffee houses will continue to flourish as they meet the needs of a society where the speed of change is only accelerating and the need for a predictable place to have a stimulating pick-me-up will only increase.

· · ·

New and Threatening Becomes Acceptable and Mainstream

February 27, 2007

Recently I have been thinking about the process whereby something that initially is perceived as dangerous to society ultimately becomes a part of the cultural mainstream. New is often perceived as threatening. Its newness is not understood, so, if it can't be understood and fit into the status quo, then it must be bad.

This thinking was triggered several weeks ago when reading an editorial in *The Economist* about the need for an age rating for video games similar to the age ratings of the motion picture industry. The thrust of the article was that something new is not necessarily bad and in need of banning; it just might need some social rating system. The article mentioned some past cultural innovations that were initially regarded as bad or even evil.

In the 18th century there was something that began to get wide acceptance that alarmed those who support the status quo. It was thought that it would poison the mind and corrupt the morals of the young, letting them immerse themselves in dangerous worlds of fantasy. What was it? The novel.

In the early part of the 19th century, waltzing was condemned as a cultural phenomenon that encouraged promiscuity. In the early 20th century motion pictures were called evil and destructive of social interchange. Those of us who are baby boomers can vaguely remember when rock and roll was something that would turn young people into devil worshippers.

As a parent, I remembered all of this as my son grew up through his teenage years an avid player of video games. While the games held no great appeal to me, I let him show me what so absorbed him. I was concerned that video games might not be the best use of his time or that they might make him less socially integrated. I, however, did not tell him that the games were bad, only that they had to be integrated with the rest of his life.

Politicians, although they don't intend to, help us realize when something new is not as bad as they lead us to believe. I remember when a certain senator from New York came out against "violent video games" and suggested that our youth be protected from them. She was not the only politician who had climbed on the moral-outrage bandwagon concerning video games. Politicians are always self-described protectors of "family values" because they think it gets them votes. What struck me about this politician's stance was that here was a politician who complained about our 18-year-olds being subjected to fantasy violence in video games at the same time she supported 18-year-olds going to kill people in Iraq using real violence.

In the 1950s the same politicians who called rock and roll the music of devil worshippers were the ones who thought nuking tens of millions of people because they were communists was a perfectly acceptable moral ground on which to stand. When John Lennon made his accurate—and critical—analysis of pop culture by saying, unfortunately, the Beatles were better known than Jesus, the politicians and religious leaders whipped their constituents and parishioners into a frenzy of record-burning. So when politicians or self-aggrandizing preachers speak to their constituents about the new evil of _____, you can almost rest assured that decades later what was so evil will become an acceptable part of the mainstream.

It is humorous that what created devil worshippers we now listen to in elevators and at Super Bowl halftime shows. Have we all become lovers of Satan? It is amusing that films were going to destroy social interchange; how many animated discussions have you had recently about films you loved? So when politicians start ranting about the violence of video games, ask them what they think about Iraq, global warming, and universal health care. Then, when they start their shucking and jiving, tell them to come back to you with their moralizing about the new evil on the cultural horizon once they have tackled the issues that affect the health of all of us.

• • •

Water

March 2, 2007

A few years ago I started the process of buying a second home in a warm part of the United States. Living in Chicago, I wanted to find a place that, through the years, would be where I would spend an increasing amount of time during the winter months. The first step in this process was looking at the various real estate Web sites that displayed listings in the Southwest and in Florida, where the weather usually stays above freezing.

The first thing I experienced was sticker shock. In the few years since I had last looked at prices for second homes in places like Arizona and Florida, the prices seemed to have doubled. This made me accelerate my search. I came into this process with a bias toward Florida because of a lifelong history of visiting the state for a number of reasons, mainly vacations and family. That being said, I have always liked the stark spiritual aspect of the desert, so I carefully looked at Arizona in particular and also Nevada.

There was, however, one thing that kept nagging at me about the Southwest: water. During the 1990s and early part of this decade I started to see that there was a developing scarcity of water in southern California, Nevada, and Arizona. Water rationing and contentious relationships between states regarding water from the Colorado River all grew dramatically during those years. The first reason was that unchecked real estate development and sprawl were covering what was essentially desert. The second reason was the stated belief by government officials and real estate developers that the region was suffering from an unusual number of droughts and that all would return to normal in a few years. So the general sense was that there was increasing usage during a time of droughts.

A convenient but not, as it turns out, an accurate analysis. Last week the research arm of the National Academy of Science released a study that basically says what had been characterized as droughts were, in fact, the norm based on historical analysis.[1] The water allocation agreement negotiated in 1922, called the Colorado River Compact, was based on river flow records dating back to the 1890s. That agreement assumed that the annual river flow was 16.4 million acre feet—enough to cover 16.4 million acres with a foot of water. Well, as it turns out, the early part of the 20th century was unusually wet, and it had been assumed in recent decades that the actual river flow was 15 million acres. This new study suggests that a more realistic number is 13 million acre feet, the level boosters had categorized as "droughts." The "droughts" therefore are the norm.

The National Academy of Science report notes that the river basin is 240,000 square miles in Wyoming, Utah, Colorado, New Mexico, Arizona, Nevada, California, and Mexico. This is a region that has seen rapid population growth in the past few decades. The report said that this growth has been sustainable because of the building of dams and reservoirs but that this activity is basically over. The Academy stated that global warming will only make matters worse. The report goes on to say that "there is going to have to be some kind of reallocation of who gets the water." Now that phrase raises all kinds of issues. Who will have the power to decide? Will the federal government have to step in to keep the states from warring with each other? Will there be laws against lawns, fountains, and daily showers? How much will water cost in 10 years, and will it be available? Will large desalination plants have to be built so the oceans can keep humanity alive?

We all have heard that you can live for weeks without food, days without water, and minutes without oxygen. Water is about human survival. The *Mad Max* movies portray a post-apocalyptic world where gasoline is scarce, but, if you don't have gas, you can survive. Can you imagine the movie about scarcity of water?

I certainly don't mean to be apocalyptic here. I just clearly see that the Southwestern United States has a developing problem that is real and is not being addressed. It probably won't be until there is prolonged rationing and states get ugly with one another about water. This is all going to happen during the next 10 years. Since I intend on living longer than that, I bought a place in Florida.

• • •

Water Redux

April 7, 2007

About a month ago, I wrote a column entitled "Water," which suggests water will become an increasingly precious resource in the Southwestern United States and that disputes will occur between states and other regulatory entities over rights to the water of the Colorado River. It was therefore no surprise to see a huge front-page story in the *New York Times* a few days ago on the topic.[2] The front-page picture was of a fishing pier jutting out into the air since Lake Mead was 80 feet below "normal." Welcome to the new normal.

The two driving forces that are making water so much scarcer are unchecked population growth in the Southwestern United States and the fact that, according to scientific evidence, what had been thought of as prolonged droughts were, in fact, becoming the new normal. This means that everything about water will need to be revisited and rethought: usage, recycling, legal interpretations of water rights and ownership, escalating prices for water, and a need for fundamental perceptual change on water and its usage. Welcome to the 21st century when we have finally come to the crossing of inevitable trend lines. These are the ever upward trend line of population growth and uncoordinated real estate development and the trend line of limited resources and climate change.

Water is a life source. Food, water, and oxygen are three things that are essential for human life and all other life on this planet. The first level of disputes will be between the governing bodies of humanity. These are already occurring as Western states sue one another over water. Then there will be new regulations of use, followed by attempts to both reuse water and find new sources, such as desalination plants, to increase this reusable resource. Then there will be the more difficult issues of adjudicating human use. What is the hierarchy of usage—drinking, agriculture, cleaning, cooling, lawns, fountains—and who will have the authority to regulate and decide? Finally, the morally difficult ground of deciding whether human need supersedes that of other species, both plant and animal. In final form, this is called triage.

This is not a cataclysmic view of the situation. It is a description of the new normal. What used to be normal no longer is. What used to be acceptable no longer is. What was taken for granted no longer can be. This is life in the 21st century. The primary issue is one of perception, or, I should say, a perception that is not really a perception of what is but a past-oriented filter through which we look at the world and then quickly look away because it no longer is the way it was. In other words, we really need to start to face forward, accept what is, and redefine a great number of things. I am convinced that humanity is up to the task of solving, or at least dealing with, any of the developing problems in the world. Whether it is global warming, the desperate need to develop alternative and renewable sources of energy, or the reinterpretation of water use and reuse, we can find our way. What we cannot do is wait, which is what we have a great collective tendency to do.

As individuals, we can act out of love. As members of large groups or of a species, we tend to act out of fear. It sometimes feels as though the only way we mobilize is to think about situations that create fear: not enough water, not enough food, not enough clean air to breathe. That may be the first step. The next step, and the one we need to take, is to accept what is and in a positive and increasingly global way reorient our thinking, change our behavior, and focus on innovation and breakthrough technology. In other words, what we have always done throughout human history. The key difference, as evidenced by the increasing scarcity of water in the Western United States, is that we now live in an age where a fundamental truth is the finiteness of spaceship earth.

• • •

A 20th-century Habit

May 15, 2007

Last week it was reported that the ratings board of the motion picture industry is now going to factor in cigarette smoking as part of the overall rating of a film. Films with excessive smoking will now certainly get a PG-13, if not an R, rating. The goal is to cut down on teen smoking, and there is a clear correlation between the glamorization of cigarette smoking on screen and people smoking in real life.

While this development is certainly to be applauded from a public health point of view, it does seem to be off the mark if the goal is to lessen unhealthy behavior in young Americans. Excessive drinking, use of guns, corporate theft and deceit, and physical and sexual violence are also bad for this country's health, and they are also widely depicted on the big screen. It is absurd to think that a scene depicting gun violence or a robbery might get a less restrictive rating if the actors are not smoking.

This news did get me thinking about cigarette smoking, but from a more historical point of view. It could be argued that, in the United States, cigarette smoking is a habit largely contained in a single century. At the beginning of the 20th century cigarette smoking was not widespread, in the middle of the century it was very common, and at the end of the century it was in rapid decline. In 1900 there were 2.5 billion cigarettes sold in the United States, which is 54 per capita among people 18 or over. Fifteen years later, just prior to World War I, the numbers were 17.9 billion and 285 per adult. In 1920 those numbers jumped to 44 billion and 665 per adult. Clearly the war helped to greatly increase smoking.

The 20 years from 1920 to 1940 saw a tripling in consumption with 182 billion cigarettes sold for a per-capita number of 1,976. Not coincidentally, those 20 years saw the explosive growth of the new entertainment medium, the movies. It was a rare movie produced in those days that did not have smoking on screen. World War II created another upsurge in smoking, as millions of GIs picked up the habit to temper the boredom and stress of combat. The 1945 numbers jumped to 341 billion and 3,449 per capita, or roughly half a pack a day for every person over the age of 18.

The 20 years from 1945 to 1965 were the zenith of cigarette smoking in the United States. This was due both to it having become a socially acceptable practice and having been aggressively advertised on television. Tobacco advertising was one of the biggest product categories during this time, the golden years of network television. Dancing cigarette packs, the Marlboro cowboy, and cigarette-named programs such as the "Camel Cavalcade of Sports" were everywhere. Even the reigning sports figures of the day, Major League Baseball players, endorsed cigarette brands. The 1965 per-capita number of 4,259, or 213 packs for every person over the age of 18, was the highest number ever in U.S. history. This number steadily declined to 2002, when it was 1,979, about the same number as in 1940.

Clearly there are still hundreds of billions of cigarettes sold in the United States today. However, the downward trend is clear. Smoking is no longer socially acceptable. Smoking in bars and restaurants is now illegal in 30 states, with several more ready to pass legislation. This is an entirely different environment than when I was growing up with an ashtray on practically every restaurant table in America. Over the next few decades smoking in the United States will continue to decline and by mid century could well go back to the levels of the early 1900s.

What I find interesting is that, primarily due to population growth, total global consumption of cigarettes is increasing, that less developed countries—which currently have the lowest per-capita consumption— are increasing at the greatest rate, and that almost 40 percent of all ciga- rette consumption is by the Chinese. That being said, the rate of growth globally has slowed over the past 10 years. Given the dynamics around global warming, agricultural food production, and the demands that to- bacco puts on the land, it is probable that in the next two decades total consumption of cigarettes globally will begin to decline significantly. I would expect that by the end of the 21st century cigarette smoking will be looked on as a habit of the past.

Once again, the United States is leading the way and, regardless of ratings, in this case, that is a good thing for the health of humanity.

Time Capsule for 2057

June 18, 2007

Last Friday, June 15, 2007, a 1957 Plymouth Belvedere was lifted out of its underground vault near Tulsa, Oklahoma. It had been buried on June 15, 1957, both to commemorate the 50th anniversary of Oklahoma becoming a state and to serve as a time capsule for the 100th anniversary in 2007. This led me to immediately think about what might be put in the ground today that would be unearthed in 2057.

First, some interesting facts about the unearthed Plymouth. The car was buried in a structure built to withstand a nuclear blast. When the car was unearthed, it was discovered that this structure was no barrier to groundwater, which had seeped in and converted the dirt around the car into mud, making it look like a victim of a flood. This made me think about all the nuclear fallout shelters that were built in the late 1950s and early 1960s, when a nuclear war with the Soviet Union was a real perceived threat. An ever-present threat far greater in scope than the terrorist events we are fearful of today. Well, since radiation moves quickly into water, it looks like the shelters that were going to save the survivors of a nuclear holocaust wouldn't have done much good. This suggests that our general perception of our ability to protect against bad events can be woefully overconfident.

The time-capsule aspect of the Plymouth was of obvious interest. The car had been buried with 10 gallons of gasoline, in case that type of fuel would be obsolete in 2007. Even in the heyday of big automotive iron there was a sense that gasoline might be a transitory fuel source. We are starting to realize the wisdom of that view today. In the time capsule there were the obligatory civic records, historical documents, an aerial photo of Tulsa in 1957, a 46-star American flag, and a list on microfilm of all the contestants who guessed what the population of Tulsa might be in 2007 (it's 390,000). There were also cigarettes and cans of Schlitz beer, that best-selling brand of the time. Cigarette usage is now in steady decline, and whatever happened to Schlitz beer?

So what would be put in the ground today to be unearthed in 2057? If it was to represent the dominant aspects of American life, the vehicle would be an SUV. It would be filled up with gasoline as there might not be much available in 50 years. Inside the SUV would be a standard flat screen TV, a bunch of remote controls, a six pack of Budweiser, advertisements for super-sized fast food (the food itself wouldn't last), pictures of McMansions, sports jerseys, a sampling of DVDs, a Blackberry, and a laptop.

If we wanted to look somewhat more forward-thinking, the car would be a plug-in hybrid, and we could feel confident it could be plugged into the electric grid in 2057 and be operational. Inside the car would be an Internet-ready HD flat screen TV, a yoga mat, a Starbucks mug, a touch screen tablet notebook computer, an iPod and iPhone, an e-book, a map of the U.S. coastline, and pictures of solar-paneled houses constructed with recycled building products.

Both of these paragraphs describe substantial parts of the American population. One view of America would be the dominant cultural view, stuck in the present and recent past. The other view would be the emerging cultural view of simple, tactile, user-friendly electronics; small cars and houses that use renewable energy; and an acknowledgment that climate change is ahead. The urge would be to bury the artifacts that represent where we are going, so we don't look quite so stupid. Think about it. What would the people in Tulsa in 2057 think of a huge SUV that gets 10 miles to the gallon of—what was that called?—gasoline, pulling into the driveway of a 6,000-square-foot house heated and cooled by fossil fuels with a big watered lawn in front? Would they be angry at what we've done? My immediate feeling is that the future residents of Tulsa would look more kindly on us if the car was a small hybrid pulling into a small house covered with solar panels and surrounded by natural vegetation.

There are two points to be made here. First, we are living in a time of rapid and radical change, so that, even as we look around our own culture, we see great movement from what was to what will be. Focus on consumption moving toward renewable. A trend from large to small; from traditional, mechanical interface to high-touch, intuitive interface. From a wasteful use of natural resources to a reliance on electronic displays and connectedness. Second, even what we think is so cutting-edge today will be quaint in 50 years. A car made out of metal? A hybrid car that burns fuel? Beach homes? An e-book reader that only holds 100 books?

The amount of change that has occurred in the last 50 years is nothing short of amazing. It is in fact a greater amount of change than in any 50-year period in human history. I am firmly convinced that the amount of change in the next 50 years will dwarf the changes of the past half century. That is both exciting and somewhat scary. It points to the fact that no matter what we put in a time capsule this year, it will seem nostalgic and perhaps puzzling to the residents of Tulsa in 2057.

. . .

Expanding the Definition of Life

July 10, 2007

I have always been in the camp of those who think there is life elsewhere in the universe. Statistically, the universe is too vast, practically beyond human comprehension, for there not to be some other form of life elsewhere. Those who have argued otherwise always come from the point of view that earth and its biosphere are unique and have a definition of life that is completely earth-centric.

It was therefore with great interest that I read the report published last week by the National Research Council.[3] This report suggests that life with an alternative biochemistry to that of life on earth may be possible elsewhere in the universe. It went on to say that the search for extraterrestrial life should be broadened to consider this possibility and recommended research and missions in which the federal government should invest to increase our knowledge in this area.

Using the phrase "weird life," the Council suggests that "the fundamental requirements for life as we generally know it—a liquid water biosolvent, carbon-based metabolism, molecular system capable of evolution, and the ability to exchange energy with the environment—are not the only ways to support phenomena recognized as life." The chair of the committee that published this recommendation, John Baross, professor of oceanography at the University of Washington said, "Our investigation made clear that life is possible in forms different than those on earth."

The assumption that "life" should be defined by what we know about life on earth has always impressed me as incredibly parochial and naïve. Who are we to think that all life in the universe must be like us and what we know? The history of humanity and of science in particular is the constant expansion of knowledge that breaks through and expands traditional definitions of the physical world. Seven hundred years ago, as we walked and rode horses across the earth, it was clear to everyone that the world was flat. That was our perception and definition.

The interesting suggestion in the Council's report is that a narrow, earth-centric definition of life might well mean that we will completely miss finding life because we are looking for it through a too-narrow definition. To assume that all life uses the same biochemical components as on earth means that scientists have artificially limited the scope of where extraterrestrial life might be found. For example, to limit the search for life elsewhere to planets or moons that have water and temperature ranges similar to earth may well be excluding large parts of the universe that do in fact have some other form of life. To again quote Baross, "It is critical to know what to look for in the search for life in the solar system. The search so far has focused on earth-like life because that's all we know, but life that may have originated elsewhere could be unrecognizable compared with life here. Advances throughout the last decade in biology and biochemistry show that the basic requirements for life might not be as concrete as we thought."

This is a paradigm shift in the definition and perception of life. Life on earth may not be anything like life on other planets or moons in the universe. Life could be anywhere and could take any shape and have a completely different biochemical composition than life as we know it. This means that future space missions must increase the breadth of exploration for extraterrestrial life. The report from the Council made a number of suggestions along these lines. Since this report was sponsored by NASA, I can only hope that it will be used to expand the vision of space exploration. While it is important to search for other places than earth that might be hospitable for human life, it is even more important to look for life as we might not know it.

· · ·

A Happiness Index

September 25, 2007

Throughout the entire course of human history, there has been consistent reference to happiness. Many philosophers have concluded the fundamental goal of a human life is to be happy, to find and share happiness. This thread exists from the earliest writings to the present day Dalai Lama. Perhaps the most succinct advice came from the great 20th-century spiritual teacher Meher Baba, who said, "Don't worry; be happy!" Twenty years after Baba's death, Bobby McFerrin recorded a wonderful song in honor of this simple, reduced prescription for how to lead one's life.

The quest for happiness, the definition of happiness, the enjoyment of happiness, the meaning of happiness is a through line of cultures around the world. In just the last two years there have been several best-selling books published on the subject and a number of magazine cover articles. Happiness as a subject is more popular than ever. It seems pretty obvious that people want more than they have. Type the word *happiness* into Amazon.com's search, and you get 214,554 titles (as of today). So people are on the hunt for happiness.

It has always struck me as odd that current cultures and governments do not focus on happiness. If happiness is what we all want in our lives, if being happy is the meaning of life, if politicians want the voters to be happy, then why isn't there a national happiness index? Sure, there are lots of polls and research done on the mood of the consumer. Sure, there is a lot of correlative data about people being happier in good economic times rather than in bad economic times. This, however, is mostly limited to economic considerations. True, that is a part of happiness for most people, but to equate happiness solely to economics seems incredibly narrow.

Think about the national indexes that are so closely monitored in the United States. The GDP (gross domestic product), the GNP (gross national product), the CPI (consumer price index), economic indexes all. What are the indexes that get reported every night on the news? The Dow Jones Industrial Average, the NASDAQ, and the S&P 500, all measurements of equity pricing. These are diligently reported every day, usually with value words attached: "it was a good day on Wall Street," or "it was not a happy day on Wall Street." Growing up in this type of culture, it is no surprise that so many people conclude that having money is the key to happiness.

Where is the NHI (national happiness index)? Is happiness in the United States up or down this month? How is the NHI trending as we move into an election year? If the goal of humanity is to be happy, then why don't we have governments that set policy toward the goal of an ever-rising NHI? Well, the first obvious reason is that we, as a people and certainly as politicians, couldn't begin to construct a penetratingly accurate index. That is exactly the point. If the national dialog were focused on what should go into the NHI, wouldn't that be a healthy discourse that might lead somewhere positive?

We could make some assumptions here about the NHI. If it is up, then crime, war, recession, congestion, pollution, and bad weather are down. If it is down, then politicians are at risk. Politicians would be focused on an ever-increasing NHI. Sounds like a plan to consider.

As a futurist, I am always looking into the future, trying to see the way it is going, the way it might go, and the possibilities that will become probabilities. I cannot think of a reason why people, cultures, and governments should not start thinking about an NHI and move toward that being a barometer of society, of government, of leadership. I am quite serious.[4]

• • •

2007: Looking Back and Looking Forward

September 27, 2007

Recently I was struck by the number of anniversaries of significant events that have been acknowledged this year. This past summer was the 40th anniversary of the "Summer of Love." August was the 60th anniversary of the independence of India and Pakistan. This week marked the 50th anniversary of the desegregation of public schools in Little Rock, Arkansas. This year is also the 10th anniversary of the opening of the Guggenheim museum in Bilbao, Spain. Next week is the 50th anniversary of the launch of Sputnik. All of these were very significant events.

Why is a futurist taking a look back on significant events? The accelerating speed of change is the reason. It is clear that in the past 200 years the speed of change has been accelerating. During the 1800s, the first full century of the Industrial Revolution, the rate of change was noticeably faster than in the 1700s. The amount of change that occurred in the 1900s dwarfed that of the prior century. The speed of change coming into the current century is much faster, perhaps 10 times faster, than it was coming into the last century. In the Shift Age, where we are now, the speed of change has literally become part of our environment.

What this means is that the next 10, 40, 50, and 60 years will encompass more change, more innovation, more acceleration than in the same amounts of time looking back to the last century.

The transformation of India in the last 60 years has been amazing. At independence, India was a poverty-stricken, agrarian economy with a rigid caste system. While still suffering great amounts of poverty, India is now the most populous democracy and the 12th largest economy in the world. It leapt into the Information Age in such a way that it is the back office and customer service center of the world. What will it look like in 2067? It is almost impossible to imagine.

Triggered by the landmark *Brown v. Board of Education* Supreme Court ruling, the forced integration of Little Rock schools 50 years ago ushered in the era of the federal government-supported civil rights movement. The emergence of Dr. King as a great moral leader, the march on Washington, D.C., and the Civil Rights Act of 1964 all quickly followed. There is no question that racial issues are still on the front pages today. We have come an incredibly long way, but we clearly have a way to go. What will equality and race relations look like in 2057? I can't help but think that it will be quite different than it is today.

Think about the cultural revolution that began during the "Summer of Love" in 1967. American culture and European culture were transformed. Music, art, fashion, sexual mores, and hairstyles changed dramatically. Drug use, political protests, cause-related demonstrations, meditation, and a changing concept of one's place in the world and role in life brought about cultural and political changes that reverberate still. There has been more cultural change in America in the last 40 years than in any similar period of time in our country's history. However, given the accelerating speed of change, the cultural changes that will occur between now and 2047 will be even more transformative. Hold on to your hats!

In 1997, when the Frank Gehry-designed Guggenheim museum opened in rusty, old Bilbao, Spain, it transformed the way cities could reinvent themselves during the transition from one age to another. There has been an explosion in the building of either new art museums or large additions to existing ones. It seems like every major city in the world has decided to make some sort of image-enhancing investment in a new museum or cultural edifice. In addition, the elevation of architecture and the star architect can be seen all over the world. Just look at the skyline of Shanghai or Dubai. It is probable that the changes around the world in this area for the next 10 years will match and exceed the last 10.

Please stop and reflect on the changes and the rapidity of change that we have experienced in the past decades. Then look ahead, and embrace the concept that this recent past is only a comparatively slow prologue to the decades ahead. Fasten your seat belts.

NOTES

Chapter 2: The Threshold Decades

1. eTForecasts, "Cellular Subscriber Forecast by Country," eTForecasts, http://www.etforecasts.com/products/ES_cellular.htm; eTForecasts, "Internet User Forecast by Country," eTForecasts, http://www.etforecasts.com/products/ES_intusersv2.htm; Donald D. Spencer, *The Timetable of Computers: A Chronology of the Most Important People and Events in the History of Computers* (Ormond Beach, FL: Camelot Publishing, 1997).

2. See note 1.

3. Moore initially used 24 months and then dropped it to 18 months.

4. eTForecasts, "Cellular Subscriber Forecast by Country," eTForecasts, http://www.etforecasts.com/products/ES_cellular.htm.

5. See note 4.

6. eTForecasts, "Internet User Forecast by Country," eTForecasts, http://www.etforecasts.com/products/ES_intusersv2.htm; Internet World Stats, "Internet Usage Statistics: Usage and Population Statistics," Internet World Stats, http://www.internetworldstats.com/stats.htm.

7. See note 6.

8. See note 6.

9. eTForecasts, "Worldwide PC Market," eTForecasts, http://www.
   etforecasts.com/products/ES_pcww1203.htm; Marshall Brain,
   "How Microprocessors Work," HowStuffWorks, http://computer.
   howstuffworks.com/microprocessor.htm.

10. See note 9.

11. See note 9.

12. See note 9.

13. MediaPost Publications, "Average Number of TV Channels Re-
    ceivable," MediaPost Publications, http://publications.mediapost.
    com; BookWire, "U.S. Book Production," BookWire, http://www.
    bookwire.com/bookwire/decadebookproduction.html; U.S. Cen-
    sus Bureau, "The 2007 Statistical Abstract," U.S. Census Bureau,
    http://www.census.gov/compendia/statab.

Chapter 3: The Shift Age

1. When first developing the concepts central to this book, I tried to
   find a word to describe the new electronic connectedness as an extension of the human brain. Familiar with the words *biosphere* and
   blogosphere, I came up with the word *neurosphere* to represent this
   new, rapidly developing phenomenon. Several weeks later, while
   making a purchase on Amazon, I was surprised to see *Neurosphere:
   The Convergence of Evolution, Group Mind, and the Internet* by Donald P. Dulchinos (York Beach, ME: Weiser Books, 2005) in the
   "if you buy this book, you might like this book" list. Of course, I
   purchased and read the book. Though the use of the term and the
   themes of our respective books are different, Dulchinos and I live
   in the same general philosophical neighborhood. Unbeknownst to
   me, Dulchinos, evidently by just a few months, had first coined the
   term *neurosphere*, so credit must go to him.

2. eTForecasts, "Cellular Subscriber Forecast by Country," eTForecasts, http://www.etforecasts.com/products/ES_cellular.htm.

3. eTForecasts, "Internet User Forecast by Country," eTForecasts, http://www.etforecasts.com/products/ES_intusersv2.htm.

4. http://www.magazine.jaring.my/2003/february/index_stay. html?id=218&month=february&year=2003.

5. Cisco Systems, "The Exabyte Era," Cisco Systems, http://www. cisco.com/application/pdf/en/us/guest/netsol/ns537/c654/cdccont_ 0900aecd806a81a7.pdf.

6. eTForecasts, "Computers-in-Use Forecast by Country," eTForecasts, http://www.etforecasts.com/products/ES_cinusev2.htm.

7. U.S. Census Bureau, "World Population Information," U.S. Census Bureau, http://www.census.gov/ipc/www/idb/worldpopinfo.html.

8. United Nations Population Division, *World Population 1950–2050: The 1998 Revision* (New York: United Nations, 1998).

9. A. N. Whitehead, *Symbolism: Its Meaning and Effect* (New York: Macmillan, 1927), 88.

10. Chris Anderson, *The Long Tail: Why the Future of Business Is Selling Less of More* (New York: Hyperion, 2006).

Chapter 4: Going Global

1. World Intellectual Property Organization, "Statistics, Data, and Indicators," World Intellectual Property Organization, http://www. wipo.int/ipstats/en/statistics; Global Insight, "China Set to Take the Lead in Global Manufacturing," Global Insight, http://www. globalinsight.com/Perspective/PerspectiveDetail9537.htm; John Hunter, "Top 10 Manufacturing Countries," Curious Cat, http:// management.curiouscatblog.net/2007/01/28/top-10-manufacturing-countries; National Commission to Review the Working of the Constitution, "Report of the National Commission to Review the Working of the Constitution," Ministry of Law and Justice (Government of India), http://lawmin.nic.in/ncrwc/finalreport.htm.

Chapter 5: Technology and Transformation

1. Rachel Carson, *Silent Spring* (Boston: Houghton Mifflin, 1962).
2. Barnaby J. Feder, "Teeny-Weeny Rules for Itty-Bitty Atom Clusters," *New York Times*, January 14, 2007, http://www.nytimes.com/2007/01/14/weekinreview/14feder.html.

Chapter 6: Energy and Global Warming

1. Cornelia Dean, "'Dead Zone' Reappears Off the Oregon Coast," *New York Times*, August 6, 2006, http://www.nytimes.com/2006/08/06/us/06coast.html.
2. Thomas L. Friedman, "The Energy Mandate," *New York Times*, October 13, 2006, http://select.nytimes.com/2006/10/13/opinion/13friedman.html.
3. Nicholas Stern, *Stern Review Report on the Economics of Climate Change*, Government of the United Kingdon, http://www.hm-treasury.gov.uk/independent_reviews/stern_review_economics_climate_change/stern_review_report.cfm.
4. Elisabetta Povoledo, "Church on the Edge of Rome Offers a Solution to Smog," *New York Times*, November 28, 2006, http://www.nytimes.com/2006/11/28/world/europe/28smog.html.

Chapter 7: Our Automotive Future

1. To learn more about the compressed air car, see http://www.gizmag.com/go/7000, http://www.cyber-media.com/aircar, and http://www.theaircar.com.

Chapter 8: A Time of Disintermediation

1. Jeff Bailey, "One City's Home Sellers Do Better on Their Own," *New York Times*, June 8, 2007, http://www.nytimes.com/2007/06/08/business/08home.html.

Chapter 10: The Morphing of Media

1. John B. Horrigan, "Home Broadband Adoption 2006," Pew Internet & American Life Project, http://www.pewinternet.org/PPF/r/184/report_display.asp.
2. Parts of this column came from an initial Evolution Shift blog entry entitled "A Sweet Story for the Future" (see http://www.evolutionshift.com/blog/2006/06/20/a-sweet-story-for-the-future). This was then reoriented into an advertising column for *Media Daily News*, a well-respected online newsletter for media and advertising professionals and a publication of MediaPost Communications. What appears in this book is that expanded column, with thanks to *Media Daily News*.
3. Katharine Q. Seelye, "A Distinctly Modern Demise for the World's Oldest Newspaper," *New York Times*, February 5, 2007, http://www.nytimes.com/2007/02/05/business/media/05oldest.html.

Chapter 11: Culture at the Beginning of the Shift Age

1. Cornelia Dean, "That 'Drought' in Southwest May Be Normal, Report Says," *New York Times*, February 22, 2007, http://www.nytimes.com/2007/02/22/us/22river.html.

2. Randal C. Archibold and Kirk Johnson, "An Arid West No Longer Waits for Rain," *New York Times*, April 4, 2007, http://www.nytimes.com/2007/04/04/us/04drought.html.

3. National Research Council, *The Limits of Organic Life in Planetary Systems*, The National Academies Press, http://www.nap.edu/catalog.php?record_id=11919.

4. I was prompted to write about happiness when I learned LifeTwo, a great Web site I have written for, was promoting Happiness Week, based on the work of Dr. Tal Ben-Shahar, who teaches Harvard's most popular class: positive psychology, the science of happiness. See http://lifetwo.com/production/node/20070921-explanation-of-of-our-upcoming-week-on-how-to-be-happy. It is worth a look and a read. Unless of course happiness is not of interest to you.

ACKNOWLEDGMENTS

Many people have given me their professional or personal support in the writing of this book.

Professionally, I need to first acknowledge and thank my editor, Celisa Steele, a gifted editor, a talented writer, and a wise and patient woman. Her firm yet deft touch helped to make this book ever so much better. A better editor one could not ask for.

Thanks to Ben Meier, whose research work on this book has been insightful and supportive.

To Steve Mazik and his company, What2Design, for designing the book cover.

To Mike Shatzkin, my tour guide of the publishing business, who gave generously of his time and, more importantly, shared his wisdom and intelligence. One could have no better advisor in publishing than Mike.

To my agent, Jeremy Katz, a wonderful blend of intelligence, persistence, and good editorial instincts. A class act.

To Arman, Dali, and Adam at Blueliner Marketing, who first suggested I write a blog. They guided and supported me, and they are a significant part of the success of http://www.evolutionshift.com, which led to this book.

To Caleb at Tough Customer, who is providing the innovative marketing techniques he uses in the world of digital music to the marketing of this book.

To Dr. Tara Palmatier, a collaborator and editor of some of my other work, whose quick mind, sharp sense of humor, and killer e-mail address brightened many a day.

To Max Alexander, whose collaboration helped to shape some of the thinking herein.

To the folks at BookSurge for their guidance and support in the final stages of publication.

Personally, there are many people to thank. First, Dr. Henry Burnett, who, almost three years ago on a beautiful sunny drive up the Pacific Coast Highway, told me to write a book. Jack Myers, a great friend for years, my TPP co-founder, media pundit, and fellow visionary. Bernard H. Baum, my own village elder, father-in-law, and exacting editor and conversationalist. To all my friends who have been there with support and encouragement along the way: Tom Geniesse; Cynthia Ivie; Stuart Friedman; Mary Lou Wattman; Gary Delfiner; David Fox; Jonathan Black; Jeff Cobb; Marilynn Preston; Bob Labate; George Rosenbaum; Susan Jeffers; Dave Kustin; Rob McGee; Larry Swenson; Tom Opper; Jay, Kevin, Todd, Tom, and Mike from TeamWorks Media; and many others who provided the warmth of friendship.

Thanks to my son, Christopher, who gave me the greatest reason to think about the future and who showed me where I was behind the curve.

To my father, Cyril O. Houle, whose disciplined dedication to the writing of books during his life and my early years, was an image I remembered when writing this book became a struggle.

To my wife, Victoria, without whose constant support this book might not have been written. She is my muse but also provides tough love when needed.

There are a number of thinkers and writers who have influenced me and helped me to come to the points of view expressed in this book. Alvin Toffler, the brilliant future-thinker, has shaped my thinking more than anyone else when it comes to looking back and looking forward. Any book by Toffler is worth reading. Then, of course, are the other great writers who shaped our collective thinking in the last half century and influenced me particularly: Marshall McLuhan, Peter F. Drucker, R. Buckminster Fuller, and John Naisbett. Also Nicholas Negroponte, James Howard Kunstler, Thomas Friedman, Peter Russell, and Howard Bloom. Also to be acknowledged are some of the greats of science fiction: Arthur C. Clarke, Philip K. Dick, Isaac Asimov, Robert Heinlein, John Brunner, Frank Herbert, Neal Stephenson, and William Gibson.

ABOUT THE AUTHOR

David Houle is a futurist, strategist, and speaker. He advises companies on forward-thinking growth strategies that can best take advantage of developing and future trends. He delivers speeches about the future, global and business trends, and vision. During his career he has been hired and retained by companies to help them build revenue and launch new brands and products. Most of his professional life has been spent in media, entertainment, and education. He was part of the executive team that launched MTV, Nickelodeon, VH1, and CNN Headline News. He has won two Emmys and a Peabody and was nominated for an Academy Award. He writes the well-respected Evolution Shift blog (http://www.evolutionshift.com) with the tagline "A Future Look at Today." Feel free to contact the author at david@davidhoule.com.

http://www.davidhoule.com
http://www.evolutionshift.com
http://www.theshiftage.com
david@davidhoule.com